Buying Right

Buying Right

Getting Started in Real Estate Investment

Stephen A. Wayner

1987 Franklin Watts New York

Library of Congress Cataloging-in-Publication Data

Wayner, Stephen A.
  Buying right.

  Includes index.
  1. Real estate investment. I. Title.
HD1382.5.W38 1987   332.63'24   86-32474
ISBN 0-531-15524-2

Contents

TO:　ARLYNE, JODI and DEVIN
　　　There is none better.
　　　I love and appreciate you.

TO:　SYLVIA and KENNETH SAMETH
　　　SAM and EDYTHE TENDRICH
　　　BARRY WAYNER
　　　The best parents and brother
　　　a man could ever have.

TO:　YOU
　　　I thank you. You have helped
　　　me make my life a success, and
　　　through this book I hope to do
　　　the same for you.

I know I must have left out some important names—for that I apologize. Special thanks goes to the following people whose contributions over the past years have helped make this book a reality:

JOHN BECK

JULIAN R. BENJAMIN

DON BERMAN

RALPH BOYER

BARRIE R. BRATT

MRS. BRINSON

GEORGE CADMAN III

MARWIN S. CASSEL

JOHN CHILDERS

ROGER DAWSON

BRUCE ERB

PETER FORTUNATO

MARC GARRISON

CHARLES GELFO

ARNOLD R. GINSBERG

GARY D. KATZ

JOYCE C. KOKEN

NICK KOON

PETER H. LEAVY

RICHARD H. LEE

M. MINNETTE MASSEY

JACK MILLER

DANIEL E. MURRAY

JIMMY NAPIER

GEORGE ONOPRIENKO

MATTHEW PARVIS

GEORGE H. PICKAR

JOHN SCHAUB

DAVE SMITH

HUGH L. SOWARDS

DON TAUSCHER

HARRIET TUCH

KENNETH WALKER

MURRAY WAYNER

BERNARD H. ZICK

Introduction

What does it take to achieve total financial independence? A million dollars? Two million? Maybe you have to be a doctor, or a lawyer. Maybe it's really a matter of luck—getting all the breaks.

It's interesting how many people equate income level with wealth. The truth is that the connection between the two is very weak. A doctor earning $80,000 a year may live in a nice home and drive an expensive car, but he is no more likely to become financially independent than the man who picks up the doctor's garbage every Wednesday morning. The IRS will take its 33.5 percent share, leaving the doctor with $53,200—not bad, you might think. However, unless he is able to defy statistics he will save no more than 5 percent of his income. That is, he will allow his expenses to total $49,200 per year, leaving him with $4,000 to save. That's a long way from financial independence.

Why is financial independence so elusive? Why do 87 percent of all retired persons live below the poverty level? I can think of five reasons:

1. *Poor saving habits.* We are a nation of conspicuous consumers. Actually, the phrase "conspicuous
consumption" is a friendly sounding bit of non-
sense. The truth is, we are nearly infantile in our
hurry to spend every last dime of disposable income. We save less money than any other nation
on the face of the earth. We marvel at the success
of the Japanese, never considering the fact that they
put aside, on average, 20 percent of their income.

2. *Lack of foresight.* As Sam Tendrich said, "If foresight were 20/20, we'd have no need for hind-
sight." How much thought have you actually put
into your retirement? If you've thought about it at
all and you're more than ten years away from re-
tiring, you're way ahead of most of our neighbors.
When we're doing poorly we tend to believe that
things will never get better; when things are going
well we believe they'll never get worse. What a
strange concept! Especially when most of us know
elderly people who are barely getting by on their
pensions and Social Security.

3. *Lack of concrete goals.* Successful people are goal
setters. When January 1 rolls around each year,
they don't make any five-minute resolutions; they
mean what they say. Let's compare real goals with
daydreams:

Goals
- You make it happen.
- It requires effort.
- It takes time.
- It takes vision of what will be.
- True goals are written down.

Daydreams
- If it happens, it happens.
- It requires no effort.
- It happens overnight.
- It's an illusion; you don't really believe it.

- It's written only in your mind—on a blank page, which is immediately crumpled up and thrown away.

4. *Procrastination.* Do you live by the creed "never put off till tomorrow what you can put off till the day after tomorrow"? If you do, you're eligible for inclusion in the National Procrastinators' Club, whose membership would be in the millions except that most of its potential members haven't gotten around to signing up. Even when we realize that something must be done, it's easier to put off doing that something than it is to figure out what that something is and do it! Perhaps procrastination is too gentle a term; laziness, in most cases, is more appropriate.

5. *Lack of knowledge.* Here, finally, is the bottom line. Even if we know that something must be done, we haven't the faintest idea what that something is, and nobody is going to take us by the hand and show us the way.

If you're always one jump ahead of bankruptcy, with too much month left at the end of your money, it's time to think seriously about your future. Your financial future is in your hands. Success—real independence—isn't a matter of luck, or a hefty paycheck; it's a matter of common sense. It doesn't take a lot of money. In fact, many people who are financially independent started with little or nothing. What was their secret? No secret, really. They just used common sense. They realized that:

1. *You can't have everything.* You can't spend all your money and have anything left over to invest for the future. Like the story of the grasshopper and the ant, you can't play all summer and expect to have anything put aside for the winter. You *must* save, and you *must* invest.

2. *You must have a plan.* Most people who fail didn't plan to fail; they just failed to plan. Goals, plans,

and foresight are the hallmarks of greatness. Successful people set goals and break those goals down to achievable plans of action.

3. *You can't do it alone.* No one is truly "self-made." Success requires a team of experts working together. You'll never reach your financial goals by hiding your money under your mattress.

4. *It really* does *take money to make money.* It just doesn't have to be *your* money. Those who have achieved great levels of wealth did so because they realized that you can leverage someone else's money and keep all the profit. Real estate is the best example of this remarkable idea. You can buy a house for $50,000, using only $5,000—or less—of your own money, and sell that same house for $60,000, keeping the entire $10,000 profit—if you *buy right.*

That's what this book is all about. I'd like to teach you how to think like the rare breed of men and women we call "self-made." I'd like to teach you how to act like them; how to walk and talk like them; how to join their ranks.

It's my goal in writing this book to give you everything you'll need to achieve the freedom you've dreamed of. As much as I'm able, I'll take you by the hand and lead you. And when I've taken you as far as I can, I'll help you meet experts who can take you the rest of the way.

You're holding a textbook in your hands, not a novel. The course is Financial Independence 101. Your teacher is a real estate attorney, a real estate broker, and a national instructor. If you want a good grade, you'll have to read carefully, take notes, and complete every homework assignment. An A in this class won't appear on any college transcript; it won't show up on your resume. No, in this class an A will mean an end to rolling over and whacking the alarm clock, sleepily dragging yourself to the shower, and forcing your body to get to work on time. Even a B will mean vacations in Europe (or anywhere else in the world) at least a couple of times a year and a secure retirement. An F, unfortunately, is what most people are earning today. How about you? If you had to hand out the grades, what would you give yourself?

I guess by now you've noticed I'm standing on a soap box. I'm not preachy by nature, but before we get into the book proper I'd like somehow to motivate you. I want you to take a close look at yourself. A few years ago you looked ahead to adulthood as a time of great freedom and independence. Life, however, had other plans, didn't it? There were too many responsibilities, and it got so you were spending more and more time making a living and less time actually *living*. I'd like to put some life back into your living. And I can do it—with your help.

I'm almost ready to let you into class. . . . Just another word of encouragement before we start.

Remember the story of the little engine that could? How he chugged his way up the steep mountain track saying, "I think I can, I think I can, I think I can. . . ." The story endures because it is based on truth. There are two kinds of people: those who think they can and those who think they can't. They're both right, of course. If you're holding yourself back from success because you think you can't succeed, please open your mind just for a moment and consider an alternative. You *can* succeed.

Enough pre-class pep talk. Open your mind, and let's get started.

Chapter One

Investing

This chapter is the basic primer on the concept of investing. We'll look at what the word "invest" means, and how and why everyone (including you) invests every day of their lives. We'll compare investments. At the end of this (and every) chapter there will be a homework assignment. Do not take the homework problems lightly. As in most courses you faced in school (or may be facing now), your lessons will be progressive. Failure to complete an assignment at any level will seriously affect further education. The assignments will *not* be easy; every one will require time and effort. Success is rarely easy.

Investing

If we turn to the dictionary for a definition of "invest," we find among its several meanings two that are of special interest: (1) "to put, as money or capital, into some type of property, with the purpose of getting a profitable return," and (2) "to spend or commit in the hope of future benefit." The first meaning gets the limelight in most investments books, and the second is usually ignored. I think that's why people never think of themselves as investors.

We all invest. We commit our time and our money in the hope of a future benefit, don't we? Most people invest at least forty hours of their lives every week in the hope of a paycheck with which they can afford at least to maintain their current lifestyle. If we have any goals, hopes, plans, or dreams, we invest time, effort, and money.

When you buy a car you're investing, aren't you? You may not expect a profitable return on the sale of the car, but you certainly expect a future benefit as you picture yourself pulling up to a stop light and gunning the engine to let everyone know you've arrived. Or you may be investing for the simple benefit of getting from A to B and back to A again without breaking down at C and having to call someone at D to pick you up.

The test of an investment is how well it satisfies the need for the future benefit or profitable return. Put more simply, the bottom line is the payoff. If you invest a hundred hours into a walk-a-thon for muscular dystrophy, any benefit derived must be purely emotional and physical—you won't make a dime of profit.

So you're already an investor. You may have invested in a car, a house, a savings account, a coin collection, piano lessons. . . . The list is endless. *The difference between those who reach the end of their lives in poverty and those who die wealthy is in how well their investments performed.* (The wealth or poverty may be financial, emotional, spiritual, physical, intellectual, or any combination thereof; however, we'll confine the scope of this book to financial wealth.)

If we recognize the need to invest, the question is then, "What is the best investment?" As I'll point out again and again, it's simply a matter of *common sense.*

The IDEAL Investment

Real estate is the common sense investment.

Why real estate? Because there is no other investment

that allows the *control* that you have with real estate investments. *You* control the price, the terms, the potential for profit,
and every other aspect of the deal. Compare that with investing
in stocks and bonds, or silver and gold. The potential for tremendous profit may exist with those investments, but nobody in
the world can predict with any assurance what their value will
be six months from now. The markets are as predictable as a
room full of two-year-olds. Of course, if you want a safe investment you can put your savings into a passbook account,
where it will try valiantly to keep up with inflation. But I'm
talking here about making enough money to retire comfortably
on a portion of your profits.

The amazing thing about the real estate market is that it
is *imperfect,* so there is an enormous range of perceived values.
The seller, anxious to get rid of a burden, may feel that his
house is worth only $45,000. You, as a shrewd investor, know
that it could be sold for $55,000. That's a *$10,000* difference
in value! You won't find that in any other market, but it occurs
in real estate every day. If the market price of gold is $300 an
ounce, how many sellers will sell their gold for $250? Not one!
Why should they, when they know they can sell it for $300 on
the open market? Gold is bought and sold in a nearly perfect
market, and everyone in the world knows the market price. In
real estate, it is your market knowledge that will allow you to
control the profit every single time you buy and sell a piece of
property.

Real estate has often been called the *ideal* investment,
and with good reason. "Ideal" is the perfect word too, for real
estate offers all of the following:

I. *Income.* You can buy and sell your real estate
quickly, banking your profits; you can sell on a
contract and collect monthly payments over a period of years; or you can hold the good rental
properties you find, collecting income at the first
of every month.

D. *Depreciation.* Depreciation is a benefit offered by
Uncle Sam. You've undoubtedly heard that real
estate is a "tax-advantaged" investment. Even un-

der the new tax law, Uncle Sam still offers real estate investors this important benefit. Before you invest, check with a competent CPA; knowing the tax consequences of your investment before you invest can only help you make a wise decision.

What is depreciation: When you buy real estate, the building and all of its fixtures will slowly lose their value (it's estimated that the average life of a building is eighty years). This constant lessening of value is called depreciation, and it is recognized as a business expense by the IRS. The land itself, however, does not depreciate, so you must subtract the value of the land from the total price of the real estate to find the **depreciable base.** As an example, if you buy a house on a half-acre lot for $100,000, and the land is worth $25,000, your depreciable base is $75,000.

Under the new tax law, you must depreciate the residential property over twenty-seven and a half years in equal amounts each year. If, for example, the buildings and other improvements on your land are worth $55,000, you are allowed to reduce your taxable income by $2,000 per year simply because you own the property—and it doesn't matter that the market value of the property is increasing every year.

The fun of depreciation is in knowing that, while Uncle Sam is allowing you to depreciate your property, it is usually **appreciating** all the while! You bought a house for, let's say, $80,000 and sold it five years later for $120,000, and the whole time you owned it you were deducting depreciation off your income tax as an expense!

There has been an important change in the tax law regarding how the profit from the sale of real estate must be claimed. Previously, if a property was owned for more than six months, the owner could exclude 60 percent of the profit as capital gains. Effective January 1, 1988, all of the profit must be claimed—and taxed—as ordinary income, regardless of how long the property was owned. Nevertheless, real estate is still the best investment. The fact that its tax benefits have suffered doesn't make it less attractive—if you buy right.

E. *Equity build-up.* Every month when you make a payment, a portion of that money pays off part of the principal amount owed (the debt). As you pay the principal on that loan debt you are building up equity, even if the property doesn't appreciate at all. It's like a forced savings account. And the way most amortization schedules are figured, each month you will be paying a greater amount of principal, and building up equity even faster. Loan amortization will be covered in much more detail later.

A. *Appreciation.* The reason for buying most investments is in the hope they will appreciate in value of their own accord. Whether it is gold, silver, stocks, or rare stamps, we are betting that somebody will be willing to pay more tomorrow than we paid today. No other investment has real estate's track record for appreciation. In fact, no other investment has consistently kept pace with inflation.

I've heard many people say that all the really big money in real estate was made in the '70s, when inflation doubled home values in as little as five years. True, prices aren't going up at that breakneck pace, but fortunes are still being made by real estate investors through the benefit of appreciation.

L. *Leverage.* Leverage means investing as little as possible of your own money to make as large as possible a purchase. This is probably the one reason that real estate shines brighter than gold—in the eyes of an investor. Ask a gold dealer for

$50,000 in gold and he'll be happy to give it to you—for $50,000 cash. And if the price of gold increases by 10 percent, you can sell it for $55,000 and pocket the $5,000. The return on your investment, of course, will be 10 percent.

Compare that with real estate. You can buy a $50,000 house and put $5,000 (or less) down on it. Of course, you will still owe $45,000 to a lender, but the property can be making those payments with rental income. Now suppose that house increased in value by 10 percent, just like the gold, and you sold it for $55,000. What is your return? It's still $5,000 cash, but since you only had to come up with $5,000 to begin with, your return is not 10 percent; it's 100 percent! That's a ten times better return, even though both the gold and the house increased by exactly the same amount. That's leverage!

It's easy to see why someone would want to invest in real estate; it really is the IDEAL investment.

Common sense. It makes sense that real estate is the best investment for the average American, doesn't it? How many people can afford to gamble in the stock market? How many can afford to wait for a savings account to make them wealthy? The only entry barriers in real estate are time, money, and knowledge—and I'll show you where to find all three. Real estate makes sense.

What Is Real Estate?

This book will be devoted to teaching you how to purchase real estate as an investment—even with the new tax laws. Before we get any further, however, I think we should take a closer look at the basics of real estate. What *is* real estate? How is it owned, and how is that ownership transferred from one person to another? We'll start with a few basic definitions, and definitions can be (Admit it, Steve) boring. But I don't think we can talk about a subject without first agreeing on its definition.

To define real estate we have to recognize its basic characteristics. Everything can be divided into one of two categories: real property and personal property. As a general rule, personal property is movable, while real property is not.

Real estate—also called **real property**—includes land and the buildings and plants it contains. **Land** is the soil, water on the soil, the air space above it, and everything below it to the center of the earth. Land also includes anything natural or artificial that is attached to it.

Fixtures are items that would ordinarily be classified as personal property, but which have been attached to real property in such a way as to become an integral part of it. Once that happens, it becomes real property. If the item is attached to the property by cement, or nails, or any other way such that removal would cause substantial damage to the real property, it is deemed to be a fixture. Also, even if the item is not attached but the owner intended it to be a fixture, it will be considered to be a fixture.

With that definition, it is fairly easy to separate real property from personal property and to understand what is meant when someone says he or she is investing in real estate: Anything from raw forest land to a fifty-story skyscraper is real estate. If you buy the house next door, the tomato bushes growing by the side of the house, the swimming pool in the back yard, and the kitchen sink are all a part of the real property.

Since real estate covers so much of the world, I'm going to restrict the scope of this book to the realty that you, the first-time investor, are looking for: single-family homes and multi-family rental properties. Raw land is not usually a good investment for the inexperienced investor, and anything as large as a commercial office building is generally too complex for the novice investor. In fact, I don't even suggest starting with multi-unit apartments. Instead, I recommend that you begin with the same investment vehicle that more real estate tycoons used as a springboard than any other: the single-family home.

A Real Estate Transaction

I will devote this book to teaching you the steps for buying real estate *right*. By that I mean all of the following: not paying too much; making every deal profitable; getting the most out of every negotiation; and writing an offer that guarantees success.

Since this chapter is the primer, I think we should look at an average real estate transaction. You will need to be familiar with every step (if you become an active investor you will indeed become intimately familiar with every step).

We will discuss each step in detail as we go through the book, but in broad brush strokes, here is how a real estate transaction works:

1. The buyer looks for property to buy. He or she can do so by any means whatsoever, and I'll show you several methods for doing so. What type of property the buyer is looking for is strictly a matter of need: a rental property, or a residence, or just a good bargain that can be resold quickly; like any other shopping, the buyer is looking for something that will satisfy a particular need.

   The reverse side of step one is from the seller's standpoint. When a seller decides to sell his or her property, there are basically two ways to do so: with the help of an agent or by owner. The agent will advertise the property and make use of a network of agents, through the *multiple listing service,* taking the work out of it for the seller and charging a commission. If the seller opts to sell it alone, newspaper ads are usually the most effective method.

2. The buyer finds a property that seems to fit his or her needs perfectly. The next step is to contact the seller and inspect the house (land, condo, etc.). This cursory inspection is the buyer's opportunity to get a "feel" for the property and decide whether or not to pursue the deal. Preliminary negotiations

are started. Both parties get a chance to discuss the good and bad points of the property and to try to arrive at a possible price.

3. The buyer continues negotiating, looking over the property more carefully and preparing a long-range plan for it. He or she will by this time be ready to make an offer and will begin lining up financing for the purchase.

4. The buyer makes a written offer. This offer may be called simply a Purchase Offer for Real Property, or an Earnest Money Agreement and Purchase Offer, or anything else at all. Check with a Realtor, a title officer, or a real estate attorney in your area to find out exactly what form is used in your state and have a handy supply of blank forms at home.

   The written offer is the most important document in any transaction. The terms agreed to in the offer are binding— it is a contract. As the buyer you can include any clauses you want in the offer; the seller isn't obligated to agree to anything in the offer, and he or she may insist that you drop certain clauses or terms before the offer will be accepted.

   Later in this book I will give you several clauses that you should include in every offer you make. These clauses will give you almost total control over the transaction. You will be able to walk away from the deal without losing a penny, to specify where and when the closing will take place, and to set the price, terms, and conditions of the sale.

5. The seller agrees to the terms specified in the offer, or makes a counteroffer, or rejects the offer completely. If the offer is accepted, then there will be an **escrow period,** during which all the necessary paperwork, inspections, and other red tape will be taken care of. The escrow period can be as little

as a couple of days or possibly several months. The length of the escrow period can be specified in the purchase offer which is, since he or she wrote the contract, up to the buyer.

6. At the end of the escrow period is the **closing.** Both parties agree on a time and place where the closing will occur. It may take place at an attorney's office, or in a Realtor's office, at a title company, or in a lender's office. In any case, this is the last stage of the transaction, when the buyer shows up with the remainder of the down payment and everyone signs all of the legal documents necessary to finalize the deal. Transfer of title takes place, and usually the buyer takes possession of the property after the closing.

Buying real estate can be just as simple as that; six steps and you're done. Notice I didn't say *easy*. I said *simple*. By that I mean that you can learn the steps that are involved and buy houses all day long without the process ever getting any more complicated. However, it is not easy; it requires hard, careful work at each stage. This is not the best occupation for anyone who wants to get rich without any effort. But it is by far the surest way to wealth for those who are willing to learn and work.

Value in Real Estate

Buying real estate and selling it for a profit isn't a difficult idea to grasp. Nor is the idea that if you want to sell real estate at a profit you'll have to buy it below market value. The problem for new investors is the question of value. Obviously, all real estate has some value, but how do you determine a particular house's market value? The difficulty with real estate is that because there are so many factors affecting value, it's tough to pin a price tag on a property.

To keep things easy to understand, I'll use the following definition for value: When someone buys real estate, the total value of that real estate is what is paid for it—no more, no less. If one can sell it for $50,000, then that is its total value; if one can find a buyer willing to pay $55,000, then it has a total value of $55,000. There is, of course, a mythical "market value," which is the price the property would command in a perfect market, where all buyers and sellers would be in agreement as to the property's value. But since none of those conditions are met in the real world of real estate, market value is an almost ludicrous concept.

Equity

An owner's *equity* is one's share of the total value. To investors, equity is the name of the game; when they sell, their equity is their profit.

To explain equity better I'll use an example. Suppose you were to buy a house for $45,000. The owners paid $30,000 for it when they bought it, and they now owe $20,000 on their original loan. What is their equity? It is the difference between what they owe ($20,000) and what they sell it for ($45,000). In this case their total equity is $25,000.

Let's further suppose that you agree to take over the payments they are making on the existing loan (you are **assuming** the loan). That takes care of their debt obligation, and all you are left with is their equity of $25,000. You can arrange to make payments to the sellers, or you can pay them in cash (some of which you will probably have to borrow), or you can pay a portion in cash and make payments on the remainder.

Whenever the sellers agree to accept payments from the buyer for their equity, it is called "selling on contract," or "carrying back a mortgage," or "owner financing." Whatever it is called, it amounts to the same thing: The sellers become, in essence, the lenders. They are lending you their equity and you must pay them for that equity, plus interest, just as you would a bank. The advantages of owner financing are apparent: The sellers can give you a lower interest rate than the bank, and they are often likely to be less stringent when it comes to credit checks.

Going back to our example, here are the terms that you work out on paying the owners for their $25,000 equity: You agree to give them $5,000 cash and pay $20,000, plus 11 percent interest, in equal monthly payments over the next twenty years. Congratulations, you have just entered the world of real estate finance. Now for the test: Suppose you sell the house the following week for $48,000. How much equity do you have in the house?

Don't read the answer yet; take a minute and figure it out. Feel free to use a calculator, pencil and paper, or even (if you like to think) just your brain.

Got it? If you answered $8,000 (give or take a few cents) then you're on the right track. To figure out the answer, you simply took the amount you sold it for ($48,000) and subtracted the amount you owed ($20,000 for the old loan you assumed and $20,000 that you owe the original sellers on the owner-financed loan, for a total of $40,000). The $8,000 is a combination of the $5,000 cash you gave your sellers and the $3,000 difference in your buying and selling prices. Since the $5,000 was your money originally, your profit from the whole deal was $3,000—not bad for one week's work.

When you call a person who is selling his or her home for, say, $45,000, and the total of the existing loans is $30,000, you know that person is asking $15,000 for equity. What he or she actually gets for that equity and how he or she gets it is strictly a matter of negotiation.

So far so good? If you stand back a little and look at the broad subject of real estate, it's not that complicated. Don't get bogged down trying to learn everything; in another chapter I'll introduce you to experts who will handle the fine details.

Let's stop for a moment and take stock: You realize that you are already an investor, but you may need to choose a new investment—an "ideal" investment—to secure your future and achieve your goals. You know why real estate is the ideal investment, and you have a basic understanding of what real estate is and how its value is determined. So what's keeping you? Why aren't you investing right now?

Timing

Many would-be investors hang back, waiting for the right moment, like a surfer waiting for the perfect wave. Many have waited for years, mistakenly thinking they don't have the time, the money, or the knowledge, or fearing that the time just isn't right. Many waited all through the '70s, and many more will wait all through the '80s and '90s.

When is the best time to invest? The temptation is to sit back and wait for just the right moment. *Now* is always the right time to invest.

Real estate is always a good investment because it has intrinsic value that is independent of the whims of people or the vagaries of the economy. People have always needed and will always need a place to live, and the population continues to grow faster than we can build. The fact that the public's demand for housing is always outrunning the supply creates scarcity, and scarcity causes price increases.

Because of that basic law of real estate, today is always the day to invest. In other investments timing is everything. Buy gold at the right time and you will make money; buy it at the wrong time and you will lose. Real estate is simply not like that, with a few exceptions we will look at. If the market price for that three-bedroom you've been considering is $55,000 today, and you can buy it for $50,000, by all means do so. There is no need to fear that it will suddenly be worth only $45,000 tomorrow. Generally, it will either stay at its current price level or rise in value. Waiting for the economy to pick up before investing is ridiculous when you can be making money today.

The exception I mentioned is when an outside influence affects a market segment. For example, an area may be rezoned, greatly reducing the value of the property. Or a steel factory may be built three blocks from your latest rental unit.

But these can be foreseen if you have done a little homework before buying. A trip down to city hall to check developments and zoning will be enough to put those fears to rest.

One factor of investing that will fluctuate greatly, affecting your decisions, is the interest rate, which does have an effect on timing. When the current rates are high, it may be time to buy only properties with low-interest assumable loans, and when the rates are low you may be willing to find new financing. But never is there a time when you cannot invest profitably—if you use common sense.

Buying Right

You might not be convinced yet that real estate is the best investment for *you*. Many people think that they can't afford to buy property just because they don't have the time or money. You actually can invest profitably, using only the resources you have now—if you learn how to *buy right*.

The need to "buy right" becomes more apparent as we look at the meaning of the expression. It's easy to understand buying a cantaloupe right, isn't it? Or is it? First you must choose *where* you buy the cantaloupe—at a fruit stand by the side of the road or at the supermarket (and then you have to choose between supermarkets); you must be able to tell one cantaloupe from another—you must *appraise* its ripeness; you must know *market value* well enough not to overpay. All of these factors will influence your decision, and all of them combined will determine whether or not you have made a good purchase.

Comparing the purchase of real estate to the purchase of a cantaloupe is like comparing a space shuttle to a paper airplane. The theory is similar, but in practice a few more things can go wrong. Nevertheless, it's apparent that *buying right* is the basis for success in any investment. Especially when you plan to resell the object of your investment. Common sense tells you that if you pay more than market price for an item, you'll have a hard time making money on its sale.

You should by now:

1. Realize that you are already an investor, and that you must invest for your future. If you haven't achieved your dreams, you should re-examine your investments. Invest at least 10 percent of your income for tomorrow.

2. Understand why real estate is the IDEAL investment. When it is *bought right,* it requires a minimum investment of your own money, while returning the greatest profit and allowing the greatest control possible.

3. See the need for learning how to *buy right.* By studying the concepts in this book, you'll learn how to estimate market values, negotiate with sellers, and put together a winning transaction every time.

4. Be convinced that *now* is the right time to invest. Tomorrow is always over the horizon; retirement homes are filled with people who waited for tomorrow. When the time comes to retire, I don't want to have to be shipped off to a retirement home; I want to own it!

5. Understand that investing—all investing—is a matter of *common sense.*

I believe strongly in a down-to-earth, common-sense, step-by-step investing strategy that has four parts:
1. Find the best deals.
2. Obtain the proper information.
3. Structure the transaction.
4. Write the contract and close the deal.

Study this well; you'll be spending the rest of this course learning every step in detail.

Chapter One Summary

1. Everyone invests whatever resources he or she has at hand in hopes of getting a profitable return. In

fact, almost every action, from the moment we roll over and backhand the alarm clock to the moment we give in to sleep again, is an investment of time, effort, and/or money. The returns on our investments will vary widely; an hour slouched in front of the TV will cost only time and will offer a return in terms of physical and mental relaxation, while an hour looking at properties or making offers will cost time, money, and effort and will offer a monetary return.

2. Success or failure is a matter of *choice*. Those who reach the end of their lives in abject poverty are those who *chose* to invest their resources unwisely. The few that live out their lives in luxury *chose* the right combination of investments. Over 70 percent of them chose real estate. The rest started their own business (against a statistical failure rate of nearly 80 percent) or obtained their wealth through some lucky stroke of good fortune or birth.

3. Real estate is the IDEAL investment. It offers the best combination of low risk and high return available to the average investor. It is the dependable, common-sense investment. If you've ever had a car that wasn't much to look at, but that always started every time you turned the key and always got you where you wanted to go, you know what I mean. Because all five IDEAL factors add their respective returns into the pot, it's not unusual for a real estate investment to earn over 100 percent returns the first year alone!

4. Real estate is a basic, stable commodity that will always be in demand. It will always have value, and the value of a particular piece of property is a *perceived* value based on many factors. Because a buyer and a seller will usually have two different perceived values, real estate is an imperfect market—and its imperfection is what creates good deals.

5. Now—today, this minute—is the time to invest. Real estate, bought prudently, is *always* a good investment. If you doubt it, ask people who have invested in real estate *carefully,* paying special attention to buying right, if they think now is a good time to invest. You know where they live: in that big house on the hill, the one with the circular cobblestone driveway that people are always calling "the mansion."

6. If you want to succeed as an investor you have to *buy right.* The key to buying right is learning how to use your own common sense to find the best deals. In the next chapter we'll concentrate on how to find the properties that qualify as good deals.

Chapter One Homework

1. Determine how much money you have made in the last ten years and track its expenditure (estimations are allowed). If your income is in the median range, you might be surprised to find that you've spent nearly a quarter of a million dollars. Where did it go? How much of it was spent on the future—invested? How much went strictly to food, clothing, and shelter? (If the answer is "most of it," you may be wearing your retirement around your waist.)

2. Budget 10 to 20 percent of your net income and 10 to 20 hours per week—for at least one month—for investing. If the numbers won't work, figure it out again and again until they do work. If you can't find the money, something has to go—some luxury you can do without for at least a month. If you can't find the time, consider getting up earlier, eating on the go, giving up a hobby, or going to bed later. The time *can* be found, even if it means a

real sacrifice of your leisure time for the next month. If you have already budgeted your money carefully and absolutely cannot find extra for investing, you're still okay; we'll talk later about methods for getting the money if you don't have it.

3. When you've found the time and the money, and have *written* a goal to invest them for the next month, put that goal where you can see it and stick to it! It'll be tough as a diet in December, but the rewards will amaze you. During the first month you'll need to put the money in a special savings account, and you'll spend the time studying the real estate market, this book, and other sources of knowledge that I'll teach you about as we go along.

Remember, this book isn't *The Wizard of Oz*. It's not a Stephen King novel, the *Reader's Digest,* or the *TV Guide*. It's not even a college textbook, filled with theory and conjecture. This book is a guide to real-life investing. I'll teach you what you need to know to succeed as an investor, but it will require your cooperation and sacrifice. If you skimmed over the homework assignment with a yawn, I hope you'll reconsider before going on. I didn't write this book to teach Stephen Wayner how to invest; I wrote if for you.

If you've answered the questions and have at least completed the first two parts of the homework assignment, it's time for Part One: Find the Property.

Part One

Find the Property

Chapter Two

Buying Right, Buying Wrong

Finding the Right Property

How do you know if *anything* is a good deal? If you're shopping for a ball-point pen, and you find one in the local drug store that is selling for $550, would you buy it? No, of course not. Why? Because $550 is way out of line with what you already know about pen prices. What if the store was selling the same pen for sixty-nine cents, but the plastic casing was cracked and the point leaked? Forget it, right? You know as well as I do that a defective pen is worthless.

A good deal in real estate is the same as a good deal in any market: A good deal is anything that you can buy below market value and resell at value. You could buy a property for 50 percent of its fair market value and sell it immediately for 80 percent of value, pocketing the difference. That's a good deal.

Product knowledge is what allows us, as consumers, to make buying decisions, from a ball-point pen to a mansion. As the price range of the product rises, we are likely to spend more time researching it, perhaps doing a little comparison shopping. On purchases above a thousand dollars, such as a new car, we will likely spend several weeks or even months studying prices and quality and comparing features, until we are ready to make a purchase.

The highest price level that most of us will ever work in is that of a house. It makes sense that we will spend months learning values and comparing prices. One or two weeks of driving around town and reading one or two books on investing aren't enough. To know if a property is a good deal, you must first learn market values well enough that you can appraise real estate without fear.

There are several methods for learning property values. The first I use is a hands-on method of driving through neighborhoods, looking for "For Sale" signs, and talking to owners. This is quite time-consuming, but when you are first learning your market, there is no substitution. Become an expert in four or five neighborhoods, rather than trying to learn values all over town. You can spend as much—or as little—time as you wish, but I suggest at least two or three full days each month when you are first starting.

The second method for learning values is through the MLS (multiple listing service) book that every real estate agent has. This book is a compilation of houses that have been listed for sale through Realtors. The book is not available to the public, but that doesn't mean you can't get a look at one. Many agents will allow you to look at old copies of their MLS books if you are persuasive enough. I've even heard it suggested that you can look in the trash cans behind realty offices for old copies. Also, if you get to know an agent quite well, he or she will likely be happy to lend you a book.

The MLS book has a picture of each house, with a description that includes the address, size, number of rooms, amenities, and asking price and terms. With an MLS book in hand, you can drive through the neighborhood and compare listed prices without having to call anyone. Again, you will be surprised at how quickly you will pick up at least a general feeling for market prices.

Before you do anything else, before you read one more page, stop now and commit yourself to actively learning real estate prices in your area. It will take time—several hours every week—but that time will be well spent. It won't cost you more than a couple of gallons of gas.

What Kind of Property?

I'm often approached by seminar attendees who, after getting fired up about investing, can't wait to buy their first shopping center or apartment complex. While I have personally invested in large multi-unit properties, I don't think it's the place to get started.

Condominiums or Townhouses

I'm not particularly opposed to investing in condominiums or townhouses, but you should be aware that there is a direct relationship between control and maintenance. With a house you will have almost total control and total maintenance. With a condominium or townhouse there will be less control and less maintenance.

Finding out exactly how much maintenance and control you will have is simple; all you have to do is ask the condominium association. With a house you have to paint the exterior and cut the grass, but it is up to you what color you want to paint it and how often the grass will be cut. In a condominium the grass will be cut for you and the units will be painted, but you will have little to say about it. You will also sacrifice control over noise, children, the quality of the other tenants—to name only a few—which will affect how easily you can resell the unit.

As an additional note: Most investors seem to prefer houses to condos or townhouses. I suspect that to a large degree it's a matter of temperament; the investor is by nature that special breed of person who likes to be in control.

Mobile Homes

Mobile homes may seem like an attractive investment to the new investor who has little cash; however, I'd like to steer you away from them. Let me explain the problems involved in buying a mobile home—especially as an investment property.

A mobile home, unlike any other type of property, will lose value every year. It may not lose much and, in fact, may even hold its value for quite a while; but over the long haul it will still lose money. However, living in a mobile home, as opposed to renting an apartment, may be a good idea; at least you will recapture some of your investment when you sell.

The second (and much more severe) problem is the park owner. Mobile homes are only allowed in certain areas in most communities, so you will need either to buy one that is already located in a mobile home park or to find a park that will let you in. In either case you are at the mercy of the park owner. He owns the land, and most park owners will not give a lease to the home owners. That means that you can be evicted at any time, for any reason—or for no reason at all. And, if you have a renter in your mobile home, the park owner must approve your renter—if he will allow you to rent your mobile home to someone else.

My advice: Stick to real property, such as single-family homes, condominiums, townhouses, and multi-unit apartments, as investments.

Multi-Unit Housing

This has been a longtime favorite of investors, and as an apartment owner I can't knock it. However, as a starting place it's a little like taking driving lessons on the Indy 500. An apartment complex *can* provide a healthy income, tax benefits, and appreciation, but the initial investment is usually quite high. We'll cover income-producing properties in more detail later in this chapter.

Single-Family Homes

This is by far the favorite of new investors, and with good reason: Bought *right,* the single-family home can provide everything you've ever wanted in an investment and more. You can enjoy monthly rental income, appreciation, and tax benefits, with a minimum investment and maximum control. For those reasons, most of the remainder of this book will concentrate on buying these wonderful money-makers.

When you're shopping for an investment house, look for neighborhoods that have a solid, all-American blue-collar feel. These neighborhoods offer the best combination of low price and high stability. There is often a high degree of pride in the home owners, since for many of them it is their first home.

If you invest in a higher priced area, you will be faced with at least three difficulties: First, the high payments will mean that you will need to demand a high rent from your tenants. Attracting tenants with enough money to pay the higher rent will be difficult, since most people who can afford such payments buy their own homes instead. Second, you will find that tenants who write resumes, jog, and drink Perrier simply can't be bothered to tighten a screw now and then. If anything goes wrong at all, you can expect a call. Third, when you try to sell the house, you are selling in the high price range, where sales are always slower; it may be several months before you can find a buyer.

The extremely low end of the housing market may seem attractive at first glance. But remember, whether you are renting the house or selling it, you will only attract the kind of people who are comfortable living in that area. The run-down section of town will often draw the very worst kind of tenants, and finding a buyer who wants to live there will be difficult.

I have had some very good experiences in blue-collar neighborhoods. If every house on the block is owned by the resident except for yours, so much the better. Your tenant isn't likely to admit that you are the real owner, and the pride of ownership exhibited by the neighbors will rub off. Your tenant will be ready, willing, and able to make minor repairs without calling you, and will likely stay put for a long time. In fact, your tenant may be the first place to look for a buyer when you're ready to sell. And if the tenant can't buy the house, you will still find it easy to resell just because of its location.

The Neighborhood

Once you've located an area that you think will be perfect for investing, you need to take a good look at it. Don't look at the neighborhood through the eyes of a money-hungry investor looking for a quick buck. Start examining the area from a home owner's perspective. If you wanted to live on this street, what would you want to know about it? Would you want to know where the nearest shopping center was? How about schools, churches, and bus stops?

Here are some questions you should be asking:

The schools: Where are they located? How good are they? (This question can often be answered by talking to a few of the people who live in the area and visiting the schools yourself.)

What colleges are in the area? How are they rated?

Transportation: Is there a bus service? Where are the bus stops located? What other forms of transportation are available (subway, taxi, etc.)?

Where is the police station and fire station? (That's a question that few buyers may consider, but if these services are close it can be a plus factor when you try to sell the house.)

What does the neighborhood look like? What is it like during the day *and* at night? (It's a good idea to drive around the area, approaching it from several angles, to get a feel for the neighborhood. If most of the yards and houses are messy and children are running out into the street in their underwear, you may have difficulty finding tenants and buyers.)

Where are the local churches located? It's an excellent idea to talk to the local clergy. They are often the best source of new tenants, buyers, and sellers, since many people will tell their minister or rabbi about their upcoming move.

Community services: Where are the shops? Is there
a mall nearby? What about entertainment; is there
a theater, a bowling alley, a skating rink?

Where are the nearest gas stations?

Where is the closest hospital?

You will no doubt think of other considerations that apply to your area. I have a friend who is also an investor, and he
uses what I think is a truly ingenious method for evaluating
neighborhoods. He has done all of the research listed above for
a large area, and he has a map of the area on a wall. In the map
are colored pins that identify all of the churches, shops, etc. He
has familiarized himself so thoroughly with each area that he
can talk to prospective buyers and tenants about the house they
are considering as though he was born and raised in it himself.

Once you've found the right neighborhood and have
learned all you can about it, take time at least once a week to
drive through looking for houses. When's the next day you have
five hours that you can devote to looking at property? Plan now
for that day. You will hop in the car and drive over to . . .
(you should have an idea of the ideal neighborhood by now).
Drive slowly and look right and left. Find those "For Sale"
signs. You will probably be surprised at how many homes are
for sale; it's one of those things you don't notice until you are
looking for it.

The homes will either be for sale by the owner or listed
by a realty company. In either case you can stop and talk to the
owner or jot down the phone number that appears on the sign.
(Many beginning investors don't feel comfortable talking face-
to-face with the sellers. That's all right, but you shouldn't have
any trouble making a phone call.)

What you want to find out when you call is the sellers'
asking price, how much they want for a down payment, and
what they would be willing to consider taking. Associate the
price they give you with the home itself. If they would be willing to let you see the house, a walk-through will give you an
even better idea of value.

You should be able to look at ten or more homes in one afternoon, and if you do that in four neighborhoods every couple of weeks, it won't take long before you will find yourself saying, "They want $65,000 for *that?* It's not worth more than $55,000, even with the extra yard space and the sprinkler system."

Keep in mind that you are only "window shopping." You can leave the checkbook at home and enjoy the free education.

Price + Location + Terms = Value

When you're trying to find a good deal, you'll have to take three factors into consideration: price, location, and terms.

Price is obvious; that's the dollar figure, such as $80,000, that the owners are asking for. They want $80,000, you know the market value is $78,000, and you offer $75,000. But price is only one piece of the pie; location and terms also affect the transaction.

Location means more than where a house is located on a particular street; when a real estate investor talks about location, he or she is referring to the desirability of the neighborhood, its projected future, even the city itself. A house at the top of the hill may easily sell for $110,000, but move it downtown, across the railroad tracks, and you'll be lucky to give it away for $50,000. That's the value of location. Identical houses two blocks apart may command very different prices. Because of the location factor, you should become an expert in a few selected neighborhoods, rather than trying to learn values all across town.

The term *terms* has been a part of real estate terminology for just a short term. (Sorry; I couldn't resist.) It refers to how the financial details of the transaction, such as the down payment, the interest rate, the number of years on the loan, and the monthly payments, are to be arranged.

For example, let's assume that you are buying a house from me. We have agreed on the price: $69,000. Now we need to structure the **terms.** I owe $55,000 to a mortgage company, on which I am paying $550 a month. The remaining $14,000 is my equity—the share of the total price that goes to me. I will allow you to assume my mortgage, which has an interest rate of 10.5 percent. The monthly payments are due for another eighteen years. I would like to have all of my equity in cash to apply to the purchase of my next property.

You are excited about the loan I am offering. If you had to get financing for the $55,000, you would be stuck with—at best—a thirty-year fixed-rate loan with an interest rate of 12 percent or more. But you don't have $14,000 cash, and even if you did you wouldn't want to give me that much of a down payment. Instead you propose the following: You will pay me $4,000 now and $2,000 a year from now as a total down payment, and you will pay the remaining $8,000 in equal payments over the next ten years with interest of 10 percent.

We disagree, but at least we have a starting point for negotiation.

What we are negotiating about are the **terms** of the transaction. When we finally hammer out an agreement, you, as the buyer, should make sure that the terms are such that you can make the down payment without paying too much up front, and the rental income from the property covers all of your monthly costs.

In my seminars I ask if anyone has property for sale. Invariably people do, and I ask them for their asking price. Someone may have a house for which he or she is asking $80,000. I tell the seller that I will gladly pay the full asking price—on one condition: he or she must agree to my terms. I'll give the seller a dollar down and a dollar every month until the loan is paid off. Agreed, the loan will never be paid off, but who cares? I'm not going to live forever, and as long as I live I can enjoy a healthy rental income from the property. I will always have *positive cash flow*—and that's what I call very, very good terms. If I were to impose one law on every investor, it would be this: *Thou shalt have positive cash flow.*

There was a time, not long ago, when it was a standard saying in the real estate world that the three most important things were location, location, and location.

Times change.

Yesterday's advice was excellent . . . for yesterday's market. Inflation was, if not constant, at least predictable: If you held onto any property in a good area for a couple of years, it was sure to double in value. Today we're faced with an often sluggish market and new tax laws, and you can no longer trust inflation to make you wealthy; price and terms must play an active role.

Consider the part that each of these aspects of a good deal plays and how they relate to one another. If your location is good but you paid too much for the property, or didn't get the good terms (low interest rate, low monthly payments), you are left with only inflation as your ally. Not good enough.

If you get excellent terms and a good price, but the house you just bought is at the end of the industrial section, between the steel mill and the auto shop, you will find it difficult to fix up and rent or sell. Location is still vital, and I always recommend finding a house in a good middle- to lower middle-income neighborhood. Another real estate truism is "buy the worst house in a good neighborhood," and it is still true. You can always improve the worst house in a good neighborhood, but you can't do much about a run-down street.

Look at all three aspects and allow them to lend their weight to one another in making up your mind. Location: Don't invest in a lousy section of town just because the price is right. Price: Don't overpay for any property. You should appraise it yourself before you consider it; you may want to have it professionally appraised before you buy it. If it's worth $70,000 and you pay $78,000, how can you expect to make money? Terms: If you can't structure your down payment, interest rate, and monthly payments to create a positive—or at least break-even— cash flow, then you need to start restructuring the terms before you close the deal. Profit is the objective, remember? If your payments are too high you will lose money every month you own the property, and you will have a tough time finding a willing buyer.

There is an exception to the general rule of never paying more than the market value for a property, and that's when the terms (the interest rate and down payment) are low enough to create a monthly positive cash flow from rental income.

To give a concrete example, I recently purchased a townhouse worth $67,000. I paid $75,000. I paid $75,000 for a $67,000 townhouse! Some investor, right? Why? Well, the location was excellent, the price was terrible, and the **terms** were the best I had seen in a long, long time.

The seller was willing to accept $5,000 as a down payment and the remaining $70,000 on a long-term, low-rate loan. The interest rate was so low, in fact, that the payments were much lower than if I had purchased the house for $67,000 and had been forced to pay the market rate for a new loan. My down payment was less than 10 percent and my monthly payments were just where I wanted them to be; if the ''selling price'' was too high it really would make no difference. Again, price isn't the only consideration; in fact, by itself price means little.

In the example just given I was able to satisfy my needs *and* the seller's needs. I was looking for terms that would allow my tenant to pay my mortgage payment, cover my management costs, and leave me with a few dollars left over each month. I was looking for positive cash flow and I found it. Why should the selling price matter?

The benefits to the seller may not at first be obvious, until you take the *needs* of this seller into account. He didn't need a great big cash down payment; in fact, he was happy to have sold the property at all. Also, he was able to sell it for more than it was worth—at least that's what the bottom line said.

On my side of the same coin, Uncle Sam allows me to depreciate my investment, and with a sales price $8,000 above the market value I can take an additional $8,000 in depreciation expense.

We both win.

I didn't actually overpay, because the excellent terms give me both a tax advantage and a low monthly payment. I may be hard pressed to convince another buyer to pay me more than $75,000, but this is an income-producing property and I'm not anxious to sell. When I do, I can offer a lower price and a higher interest rate and still keep a positive cash flow.

If the whole concept of price versus terms is still confusing, take heart: In Chapter Seven we'll talk strictly about real estate finance, and I'll try to clear away the fog that may be gathering in your mind. For now, just be content with the knowledge that the price itself is meaningless without knowing the terms. They work together, along with location, to determine how good a deal is.

Let's take what we've covered so far and try a couple of examples.

Example 1: There's a house for sale on Maple, a nice three-bedroom, two-bath with a large lot. We've spent the last two months looking at similar houses in the area, at least enough to know that it must be worth $65,000 or so. The owners are asking $64,500 with $5,000 down. There is an assumable loan with a balance of $39,500, and payments are only $400 a month. The owners are willing to finance the balance on a long-term, low-interest loan.

Let's take stock:

Price: Fair. Not a fantastic bargain, but below estimated market value. Certainly worth looking into.

Location: Good. Just the right blue-collar neighborhood, and the house under consideration only needs a little fix-up to make it as good as any other house on the block.

Terms: Excellent. With the low down payment and the low-interest loans, monthly payments will be easily covered by rental income.

Example 2: Another house, on Elm, is similar to the first. It's also a three-bedroom with two bathrooms, slightly smaller than the first house. Its owners are asking $62,900, and, after your experience in looking at similar houses, you know you could sell it for $66,000 or more. The owners insist on getting the full amount in cash, which means that you'll have to find your own financing.

Again, let's compare value factors:

Price: Excellent. You could probably offer even less than the asking price, and end up getting the house for $60,000.

Location: Good. Comparable to the location of the first house, Elm Street is another blue-collar neighborhood with shady trees, Chevys and Fords in the driveways, and children hopscotching down the sidewalk. The house is in quite good condition, needing only an afternoon of cleaning.

Terms: Somewhere between poor and downright lousy. You'll have to qualify for a new loan, which means coming up with 10 percent or more to satisfy the bank. Interest rates aren't bad, but they aren't the best, either. Plus you'll be faced with the bank's added-on costs (closing costs, origination fees, application fees, etc.) which can add up to thousands of dollars—in cash.

You've got two possible good deals. Which one is best? That depends on **you,** and the long-range plans you'll have for the property you buy. That's the next factor in finding a good deal.

Long-Range Plan

Without a plan, no property is a good deal. By the time you make a written offer, you should already have sold it or rented it—in your mind, anyway. The first example above would be an excellent "keeper"; a property that, because of its excellent terms, is worth holding onto. If, for example, your total monthly payments will be $650—including the loan assumption, your payments for the owners' equity, taxes, and insurance—and it will rent for $700 per month, you'll have a $50 monthly positive cash flow. That's $600 per year income on your $5,000 investment, plus appreciation, plus tax write-offs.

The second house is a very different example. First, you will have to come up with at least $7,000—and more likely $10,000 to $15,000—cash just to get the conventional financing you'll need. Second, the large down payment will bring your monthly payments down to a manageable level, in which you may have a positive rental income, but the return on your investment will be much lower than in the first example.

On the other hand, if you can immediately sell the house for its full retail value of $66,000, you'll recoup your investment plus a healthy profit. And if you don't have the down payment, you can probably find a partner who does (more on finding partners later). If you buy the house for $60,000 and sell it for $66,000, you can split the $6,000 profit with your partner, netting a $3,000 profit for yourself—with no money out of your pocket.

The point is, without a long-range plan of action, you don't have a good deal. *Buying right* is meaningless without having a plan to *sell right*.

Buy/Sell or Buy/Rent

When making your long-range plans (as part of buying right), you have to decide whether to buy, fix up, and sell, or buy and rent.

I have two rules for buying property that I will be keeping for rental income (as opposed to property for resale): First, I will not buy any multi-unit apartments unless the rental income will pay for a full-time manager. (And I don't recommend that you start your investing career with multi-unit properties.)

I don't have the time or the patience to play nursemaid to an apartment complex, and if the rents won't pay for all expenses—including management—I will keep looking. If you have a multi-family unit and you are not able to manage it, or if you have twenty or more units, it is a good idea to have a full-time manager. As a basic rule of thumb, if you have twenty or more units, you can probably afford to hire a manager.

Second, every single-family property I buy must be no more than one hour's drive from my home. As a manager I expect to have to deal with occasional problems, and I do not want to spend three hours driving to a house if there is a fire or flood. Also, there will be times when I want to show the property to prospective tenants, and I do not want to devote an entire day to showing one property for rent.

How far afield you want to invest is up to you and will depend on your own market. You can usually find more than enough good rental properties close to home if you learn how to look.

The only other guideline I can offer is a general comment about rental property: If the income the property produces (including any tax advantages that put cash back in your pocket) is enough to cover all of your costs **and** pays you well for your time **and** gives you a good return on your original investment, why sell it? In today's market you are much more likely to find the high income you are looking for by buying and selling homes and making an immediate profit.

If a prospective deal doesn't fit my guidelines for income property, I will either buy it for immediate resale (if the price, terms, and location are all excellent) or I will pass it up.

So far, as I've discussed buying and selling versus buying and renting, I've kept the examples simple, sticking to basic concepts of judging an investment based on only a couple of factors. I've done that for two reasons: First, so you won't be scared away; second, to remind you that successful investing requires common sense, not an MBA. Actually, before making a final decision about a particular real estate investment, many people choose to take even more into account, including, but not limited to: a comparison of the tax consequences; the net cash flow available (determined by the gross rental income less the house payments); how much you put down; and how much you paid for the property compared with its true market value. You can analyze an investment to death, but common sense should tell you to concentrate on the whole picture without getting bogged down in details.

Assuming you're ready for a more in-depth look at this important decision that you'll have to make before buying property, here goes:

Buying and Renting
(holding onto the property)

Let's look first at the pros and cons of buying a house and renting it. On the pro side, you have a monthly rental income (possibly), tax benefits, equity build-up, and a safe, usually profitable place to park your investing money. On the con side, you have management hassles (which are rarely as easy as you think they'll be); your money is tied up in one property where it may be earning you an income but is unavailable for reinvestment; and you may be passing up many opportunities for enormous profits available in quick-turnaround properties.

Buying and Selling
(for a quick profit)

Buying and selling quickly has its share of pluses and minuses also. To really do well with this investing method, you must limit yourself to the few properties that lend themselves to quick profits. To qualify, the property should be selling for quite a bit below its true market value, you should not have to make a large down payment, it should need minimum fixing up, and the housing market should be brisk enough so that you can sell it quickly. And when you do find the perfect property, selling it the same day you bought it, the profit must be claimed as ordinary income and Uncle Sam will take a large portion of it

BUY & SELL OR BUY & RENT?

Features	Buy/Sell	Buy/Rent
Tax Benefits	poor, no depreciations	good; depreciation and interest deductions
Equity Build-up	nonexistent	good, over the long term
Management	great; if you can sell quickly, you may not have to manage at all	bothersome, but often worth the effort
Cash Flow	your profit will usually come all at once—which may be a tax problem	if you've structured the deal right you should have positive cash flow
Properties to Buy	undervalued with minor fix-up that can be sold quickly at a profit—keep the down payments low	only deals in which you can structure low down and low monthly payments

for himself. Nevertheless, buying and selling quickly can generate enormous profits.

To get the best of both worlds, you can sometimes find a property selling under market value that will also allow some positive rental cash flow. Hold onto it for a year or so and then sell it. You will get some profit from appreciation, some from rental income, some more from special tax breaks the IRS will give you, and the rest from the equity the seller gave up to you. Combined, these sources of profit can add up to staggering returns of over 200 percent!

Every time you are looking at a property, you need to be thinking of the various options you have, weighing rental income and tax benefits against the profit potential in reselling. Each case will be different, and each will require a careful, thorough analysis, but once you have found the house's rental income and market value, and have estimated the tax advantages, it will be easy to decide what you will do with the property.

One of the first considerations is cash flow. Ask yourself, if I rent out this house, will the rental income cover my payments and miscellaneous costs, or will I be feeding an alligator? (*Alligator:* Real estate lingo for any property on which the payments exceed the income. So called because it eats up your money.) And if I must feed an alligator, will it be made up in tax savings and property appreciation?

Positive rental income is determined simply by the amount of your gross rental receipts less your costs, including loan payments and maintenance costs. A positive cash flow is not very common today, especially in areas where the inflation of the late '70s pushed prices beyond almost everyone's reach. Part of your own research should be a comparison of local rental rates for homes in your area. It shouldn't be hard to look in the paper under "Real Estate for Rent" or "Houses for Rent." Make a few phone calls and look at some of the houses for rent. Do your research well; what you find out will be the basis for whether you decide to rent the property or not.

It's most common for house payments to be one hundred dollars or more higher than rental rates for the same houses. It makes sense, too. The people who can afford the full house payment will probably find a way to buy the house; why should they make payments on a house without owning it? You'll find the houses that offer the best chance of positive cash flow where I've recommended you invest: in the lower middle-income neighborhoods. You will find that at the lowest end of the price spectrum payments might be low enough to give you a positive cash flow, but maintenance costs are usually quite high and the tenants you will attract may damage the living room carpets with their motorcycle tires. At the higher end of the spectrum you may have excellent tenants—when you can find people who can afford the higher rents but don't want to buy a home of their own.

Positive Cash Flow

When you find a house with a positive rental income, you may want to keep it—but not necessarily. It will depend on how much below fair market you paid, how much you paid as a down payment, how high the rental income will be, and how much time you want to spend managing your property.

Positive cash flow is the exception, rather than the rule. If the rental income does cover the total monthly costs for the property, it will be for one of the following reasons:

1. You made a *large down payment,* probably 20 percent or more, which means that your debt balance is low, which, in turn, will bring down your monthly mortgage payments.

2. You bought the house far *under market value* from distressed sellers, probably assuming a low-interest loan. If the sellers were desperate enough, they may have been willing to walk away from part or all of their equity, lowering your debt (and monthly payments) still further.

3. *Rents are high* in the area where you've invested, and in spite of paying full market price with only a small down payment, you are still getting a positive cash flow.

4. The sellers gave you *good terms* on seller financing; a very low interest rate, for example.

Now, should you keep the property and rent it, or should you sell it? That's the $64,000 question (maybe more)! Let's consider each of the four reasons outlined above:

1. *Large Down Payment.* I'd have to say, as a generalization, that you made a mistake in putting such a large down payment on the house. Each situation is unique, but I'll give you an example anyway. In this example you've found a three-bedroom house which you buy for $80,000. You know that the house will rent for $650 a month. You make a 30 percent down payment ($24,000), leaving you to finance the remaining $56,000. There is an old rule of thumb that says your house payment will be approximately one percent of the amount of the loan. As rules of thumb go, it isn't as accurate as, say, "the other line always moves faster than the one you're in," but it will do for

illustration's sake. Your monthly payment is somewhere right around $560, giving you $90 a month positive cash flow—before management expenses. Allowing $20 for minor repairs, you are left with $70. That's $840 a year for the first year, and each succeeding year it should increase due to an increase in rents.

In addition to rental income, there is a tax benefit—depreciation. The IRS will allow you to claim a depreciation expense on investment property. This deduction can save you a thousand dollars or more in the first year, which is a very important consideration. How much it will save you depends on your tax bracket, the value of the building itself, and when you bought the property. In this example your tax savings could be $1,000 or more, at the time of the writing of this book.

You haven't done too well here, have you? For a $24,000 investment you are getting a return the first year of about $1,840, a 7.67 percent return. And as the property appreciates you are building up equity. If the price of houses rises 5 percent per year, you can tack that onto your return and figure that—at least on paper—you will earn 12.33 percent the first year. That is a conservative estimate, and you might do even better, but is it really a good investment? You can probably do just as well—or better—with a smaller down payment and a slight negative cash flow, as I'll show you shortly. My advice is *never* to put 30 percent down on a real estate investment, unless the selling price is far below market value.

2. *Buying Under Market Value.* In this case you bought the same house, but you only invested $8,000; the owner was desperate to sell and sold it for $68,000. You only had to finance $60,000 of it, so your payments are $600 per month. Renting it for $650 leaves you with $50 per month, and if you again figure $20 for management your net cash flow is $30. Your tax savings will be slightly less also, but it would still be at least a thousand dollars the first year. Here again, the new tax laws work against the investor, since the old capital gains rules have been abolished; nevertheless, when there's money to be made from buying right, there's no reason to cry over lost tax advantages. We still have depreciation to be grateful for.

Your return in this case is $1,360 ($30 a month X 12 = $360, + $1,000) the first year on an investment of $8,000. That's 17 percent, and if we include the 5 percent appreciation, your first-year return jumps to 22 percent. That's more like the kind of return real estate investing is known for, isn't it?

But should you keep the property or resell it? Think about it for a minute. The advantage to keeping it has just been shown, but remember, you were able to buy a house worth $80,000 for only $70,000. That means you can very likely sell it immediately for at least $78,000, taking your $8,000 profit in cash. On an investment of $8,000, that's 100 percent profit! You will have to claim that as ordinary income, but most Americans are taxed on their income at lower rates now, which will help offset the loss of the old capital gains advantage.

I think the best thing you could do in this situation is keep the property for one year and then sell it. If the market price has appreciated 5 percent, the house should be worth $84,000, and if you can sell it quickly at $82,000, your profit will be $13,360 ($1,360 in rental income and tax benefits, and $12,000 in equity increase). On an $8,000 investment, your return is a truly amazing 167 percent! Find a mutual fund that is paying that kind of return—or any investment, for that matter.

3. *High Rents.* If you are fortunate enough to live in an area where rents are high, you may want to keep the house and collect your profit every month. The IRS will give you a deduction every year for depreciation, the property will continue to appreciate in value, and your monthly income will increase every year. The only reason you might want to sell such a property is if you are bothered by management problems or if you need to get your money out for an even better deal.

4. *Good Terms.* We've already talked about the effect *terms* have on the deal; now let's use an example.

You've found a house for sale. The seller wants $80,000, which you are willing to pay—provided, of course, that you get the terms you want. There is a $30,000 first mortgage on the property, with monthly payments of $300. You will give the seller $8,000 down and assume the $30,000 first mortgage, leaving you owing $42,000 to the seller. You will pay the full price *if* the seller will finance the $42,000 as follows: You will pay $250 per month (with no interest due on the balance) for the first five years. Thereafter, you will pay $290 per month (the balance financed at 10 percent) for fifteen years.

On those terms, what return can you expect on your investment? The property in question will command a rent of $650 per month. Allowing $20 per month for management costs, the monthly positive cash flow is $80. At first glance it looks as though you'll earn $960 per year on your $8,000 investment (for the first five years); only a 12 percent annual return. But wait! This is real estate, the IDEAL investment, and monthly positive cash flow from rentals is only the tip of the iceberg.

In the first year you should be able to save $1,000 on your taxes from depreciation expense. Furthermore, you will be paying down $250 per month on the balance you owe to the seller ($250 X 12 = $3,000), and every penny of that money goes directly into building up equity. If there is only a 4 percent inflation in housing prices for the year, tack on another $3,200 in appreciation profits. Add the various sources of profit together for the whole picture: $960 + $1,000 + $3,000 + $3,200 = $8,160. You've made 102 percent on your investment *the first year alone!* After the fifth year your profits would seem to diminish, but keep in mind that rental rates will climb every year, increasing your monthly cash flow.

IDEAL. No doubt about it.

Negative Cash Flow

Even if you buy in the right area, you will probably be faced with negative cash flow. To give you an example with numbers, I'll assume you live in Oleandor, Texas (don't look for it on the map; I just made it up). Two- and three-bedroom houses are selling for $75,000 to $80,000 in the blue-collar area, and they are renting for $500 a month. I will assume that you put $5,000 down (as a good investor you have managed to pay less than 10 percent as a down payment), leaving you with $70,000 to $75,000 to finance. Your payment will be $700 to $750 a month, leaving you with a $200 to $250 alligator to feed. As real estate alligators go, that's fairly healthy, and it will need to be fed every month.

What can you do about negative cash flow (alligators)? Well, here are a few suggestions:

1. *Increase the Rent.* This may seem like a facetious answer, but you should try to keep your rents as high as the market will allow. If you haven't done your homework well enough, you may be charging too little.

Another way to increase the rent is to sell the property to the tenant on a long-term lease option of a year or more, or to equity share with your tenant (both of these techniques will be covered in depth later). Your tenant will cover the negative cash flow while you collect the profit.

2. *Sell the Property.* This is, of course, one of the main options that we're discussing. If rents in your area are too low, you may not ever want to keep a property. You should sell it to a home owner who is willing to make the full loan payment, taking your profit in the difference between your buying price and selling price. Again, this will only work if you have bought the house under market value, preferably with little or nothing down.

3. *Make a Larger Down Payment.* This may put your monthly income back into the black, but I rarely recommend it. We've already had an example of using a large down payment to increase monthly cash flow, but you can see that there is usually a better place for your money—in more profitable properties.

4. *Do Nothing.* That's right; live with the alligator and feed it for a while. Let's go back to the first example, where you put $24,000 down on an $80,000 property. Instead, however, you will only put $4,000 down (5 percent). The smaller down payment will give birth to an alligator, but you can bank the other $20,000 to feed it.

Your $4,000 down payment will necessitate a $76,000 debt (part to the bank and part to the owner on a note), with payments of approximately $760. Since we've already found that the house will rent for only $650, you will have to cover the $110 difference yourself. Adding $20 for management gives you a $130-a-month alligator, or $1,560 for the first year.

That's not bad at all, really, because your business loss is deductible (there are limitations, so check with your CPA), and added to your depreciation expense it can mean a substantial tax savings. Depending on your own situation, the tax savings alone can pay for the alligator—Uncle Sam is actually subsidizing your investment. And as rents increase your alligator will get smaller every year. Now things are really looking good, because not only are you experiencing an after-tax break-even cash flow, but with the 5 percent appreciation that we've discussed, you will make an additional $4,000 in equity. Uncle Sam has fed the alligator and you have doubled your money!

Every single house you look at will have a different possible cash flow. The decision to buy and sell or buy and rent will have to be the result of careful market analysis. The bottom line is "What will be the most profitable—taking cash flow, tax benefits, return on investment, and long-term growth into consideration?"

Buying the Right Property

You should now have at least an idea of how to get started. The next challenge will be selecting a property that is not only a good deal, but that is a good deal for *you*. I can't tell you what kind of property you should buy any more than I can tell you what kind of shoes to wear. It's up to you; using shoes as an example, I could recommend a nice pair of steel-toe boots, but if you're a ballet dancer you're going to have problems doing the *Nutcracker* next Christmas. Likewise with real estate; you'll have to appraise your own situation: What resources do you have available?

Do you want to be an *active* or a *passive* investor? Do you have a lot of money but little time, or vice versa? Do you want to have a monthly income from rental properties that you will maintain yourself, or do you want to buy and sell quickly, taking your profit from the old buy-low, sell-high strategy?

Decide before you ever start looking at real estate exactly what you want real estate investing to do for you and how much time, effort, and money you have available to invest.

Let's look at a few characteristics of various investors and I'll give my recommendations for each:

1. Little time, lots of money

This investor is often a professional: a doctor, lawyer, architect, etc. He or she can afford large down payments and is usually looking for a good return on invested dollars plus a tax break. In the extreme, this is the ultimate passive investor.

Recommendation: Medium to large apartment complexes with a full-time management staff, or limited partnerships with an active investor who has the time but not the money.

2. Lots of time, little money

What you need is education. Once you've learned how to locate and buy good real estate, you'll have little trouble finding the necessary money. If you really have the time, think of investing as a full-time occupation; spend no less than forty hours every week looking at property, talking to owners, and making written offers.

Recommendation: Find the perfect deal; that one-in-a-million situation where an owner is willing to walk away from $20,000 equity. Later in the book I'll teach you where to find the money to buy the property. Believe me, if you have the time *and* the willingness to work, you have the best chance of succeeding as a real estate investor.

3. Little time, little money

This is where most investors start. They usually do have—or can find—the time to invest, but it's difficult. Another way of putting it is "little time, little money, lots and lots of persistent ambition." If you are in this category, don't think of real estate investing with the idea of buying block-long apartment complexes.

Recommendation: Single-family houses that are for sale by owner at drastically reduced prices. If the monthly payments and the down payment are low enough, you can keep them as rental properties; otherwise, you can sell them immediately, re-capturing your investment and making a quick profit. Avoid new homes and very old homes, and hold off on investing in large rental properties until you have finished your education.

There is a fourth possibility: that you have lots of time *and* lots of money. If that's the case, all you need is education and experience, both of which you can gain by reading this book.

Only you know exactly how much time, money, and ef-fort you have available for investing. The type of properties you buy and what you do with them must be determined by those factors.

Chapter Two Summary

1. Finding a good deal in real estate—or in any other marketable item—is impossible without first knowing values. Values can be learned.

2. In real estate, market values can be easily learned by choosing a specific area for investing and then watching the houses in that area. When a house is put up for sale, you can contact the owner or the selling agent. MLS books are another source for comparing asking prices.

3. You can invest in everything from raw land to in-dustrial complexes; however, for the new investor the single-family home is usually the best invest-ment. When bought right, it offers the best com-bination of low risk, low down payment, good terms, and high return. The best homes for begin-ning investors are those located in working-class neighborhoods.

4. The value of property is a function of selling price, location, and terms. A good deal in real estate is a combination of good price, location, and terms.

5. You must determine the profitability of an invest-ment before you buy; in other words, you must

have a long-range plan. In real estate, you will either buy and sell a piece of property or you will buy it and rent it out for monthly cash flow. The decision to buy and sell or buy and rent is based on several factors including, but not limited to, cash flow, tax savings, and appreciation.

6. Only *you* can define the expression "good deal." If you have plenty of time but little cash, you can find the deals and have someone else fund them; if you have the money but not the time, find a cash-poor investor to locate the deals; if you have little time and little money (like most people), you must budget your time very carefully and make sacrifices now in exchange for future wealth.

Chapter Two Homework

Using the schedule that you created as a part of your Chapter One homework (you did your homework, didn't you?), use the time for the following:

1. Spend at least three hours a week driving through your selected area and looking at houses. Make a directory of addresses and asking prices for future reference.

2. Talk to sellers and agents about the houses, but don't make any offers at this point. All you're trying to do is get a feel for values, so when Mrs. Brown says she's asking $89,900 you can shake you head and say to yourself, "It'll never go for more than about $85,000"—and be right.

3. Start keeping a written journal of your investing time. Record the date, the time spent, and what you accomplished. Keep this journal religiously for at least one month and then review it. If you'll follow through on this one simple task you'll be amazed at your progress

Chapter Three

How to Find It

In this chapter you'll learn the eight methods, the seven warnings, and the six commandments of real estate investing. By using the methods, heeding the warnings, and following the commandments, you should have no trouble finding good deals and succeeding as an investor.

The Eight Methods

The following methods have been tried and tested by thousands of investors before you. They work. They aren't fancy; they require only time, persistence, and, most of all, *common sense.*

Before I cover them one by one, it's important to point out their common bond. There are a few characteristics that apply to all good deals. They become apparent when we consider the situations where real estate is sold for less than market value, or where the seller is giving up a positive cash flow. If the seller was making money every month, why is the property for sale? And why would people sell their home for 50 percent of market value, when they could certainly get full price if they'd be patient? There are two reasons that good deals exist: an imperfect market and distressed sellers.

We've already discussed the first factor, the idea of real estate being an imperfect market. Sellers set their asking prices based on the urgency of their need to sell and a *guess* as to the property's market value. (Even an appraiser can only make an educated guess.) As an investor who has spent time comparing prices, your guess should be more educated than the sellers', even if somewhat less educated than a professional appraiser's.

Second, many sellers are in "distress situations," a euphemistic way of saying they are having serious problems for which the only solution is the quick sale of their property. Divorce, death, debts, and job transfers are only four of the most common causes of such distress. With the high payments that many owners face today, before they know it they can find themselves three or four months behind on their mortgage payments. The result: distress. And how do they spell relief? S-A-L-E. If the balance of a seller's mortgage is $45,000, and the market value of the home is $55,000, how much would the seller be willing to take for his or her home? Well, if foreclosure is impending, or if the seller must move within two weeks, he or she may accept $45,000 readily, happy to avoid the problems that waiting for full price would create.

Combine the distressed seller with the lack of perfect market knowledge and you get the rare "best deal." This is the one you read about in the newspapers and hear about at seminars where an investor bought a $100,000 home for $50,000 and sold it the next day for $80,000.

The following are the best methods for finding these deals.

1. Classified Ads
Probably the first place a seller will advertise is in the classified ad section of the local paper—especially the "For Sale By Owner" sellers, who want to avoid the expense of using an agent to list their homes.

Usually the wording of the ad will be your first clue as to the seller's desperation. A key word or phrase may mean "I have to sell *now!*" You can't be sure just by reading a classified ad whether or not a particular house will be a good deal, but you can often weed out the ones who aren't anxious to sell, and you can often spot the truly troubled owner.

Before I explain what to look for in an ad, why don't you take a short diagnostic test. Which of the following ads indicate a good deal to you?

1. Owner desperate! Will consider all offers. Assumable 9.5% FHA loan, seller will carry financing on 3 bdrm, 2 bth home. $59,000. 224-2345

2. For Sale By Owner: Beautiful 3 bdrm, 2 bth home in excellent location. Fruit trees, large back yard, close to schools. Only $65,000. Call 224-2345

3. Don't miss this one! Gorgeous 3 bdrm, 2 bth home in Pleasant Hills. Priced to sell, appraised $69,000, now only $65,000. Call PJ Realty, 226-2343

Did you decide which one to call first? If you said two or three, we may have a problem here. Seller number one, if he or she is being honest, is apparently in some kind of trouble. Number two may be in a hurry to sell, but if so shows no indication whatsoever in the ad. And number three is plainly trying to find a home buyer, not an investor. Also, ad number three was placed by a Realtor, so there will be a commission involved on the sale.

To sift through the ads you need to be aware of some key words that indicate a seller's eagerness to sell, and you need to know the features of a good deal. You are looking for good terms (a low interest rate, low down payment), good location, and possibly a hint of desperation.

Here are a few phrases that often appear in the ads you should be looking for:

Seller desperate; must sell; anxious to sell. Anything that indicates anxiety is a clue. Unfortunately, many sellers have caught on to the fact that such wording attracts attention and they may use it as a ploy to get more callers. A few questions over the phone should eliminate any doubt.

Low interest assumable loan; assume my FHA (or VA loan; 9% (or any other low percent) assumable loan; state loan. If the owners have a low-interest assumable loan, they will often say so in the ad. Almost everyone today recognizes the value of an assumable loan. FHA and VA loans are not only fully assumable, but they contain no *escalation clause,* so the interest rate will not go up when such a loan is assumed. These loans are real treasures, so you should call every ad that mentions them.

Will consider all offers, or other similar wording to the same effect. Most sellers will have a good idea as to the price they want for their property; the few that indicate true flexibility before negotiations even begin are showing signs of anxiety.

Low down; 5% down; nothing down. Any ad that stresses a low down payment is a good candidate for a phone call. It may indicate that the owner is willing to carry his equity on a note or that there is an assumable loan and virtually no equity. In any case, it is less money out of your pocket when you buy, so it is worth checking into.

There are other indicators that you may notice when you're reading the classified ads. Watch for any clues and follow up on them. Don't ignore an ad just because a realty company is mentioned, but be aware that the commission is usually charged to the buyer in the form of a higher price and a higher down payment.

I suggested that you invest in middle- to lower middle-income areas; that means looking for ads that offer houses in the right price range. Of course you can call every ad in the paper, but if the price is obviously too high you will probably be wasting your time.

Let's assume you've already gone through the classified

ads and have located a dozen promising leads. What's next? If you call the sellers, what questions do you ask? I'm going to make this part very easy; I'm even going to walk you through it step-by-step.

That first call to any seller is the most vital. You can use it to eliminate most of the sellers who don't have what you're looking for—if you ask the right questions.

To give you an idea of how to make the calls, I'll actually make one myself and let you listen in. Then, after I've hung up, we can discuss it. First, though, we'll need an ad. Here's one:

> Brand New, 1900 sq. ft. town home, 2½ baths, 3 bedroom, deck, patio, and much more. Buy now! First payment not due until Sept. $144,000 234-2342

Would you call? I like the idea of not making a payment for six months (it's March now), but three things are holding me back: the price, the words "brand new," and the lack of desperation. I'm looking for good investment deals, not a nice place to live the rest of my life. A brand new home is never an investment property, unless you are partners with the general contractor. The price tells me that it's not in a good rental district, and that it isn't selling below market value. On to the next ad:

> $900 down. Transferred, must sell, 1 year old 3 bedroom home 1900 sq. ft., assume 9% loan, no qualifying. Pmts. $541/month. Call Paul 489-1233 or 234-3452

This is an actual ad! If the alarms aren't ringing in your good-deal sensor, you'd better get the batteries checked. Let's call:

"Hello, I read your ad in the paper. Do you mind if I ask a few questions about the house?"

"No, go right ahead."

"Are you the owner?"

"Yes."

"And your name?"

"Lisa Peterson."

"Lisa, the ad doesn't mention a price. What is the balance of that assumable loan, and what kind of loan is it?"

"It's an FHA loan, and the current balance is $52,000."

"Oh, so you're asking $52,900 all together, right?"

"That's right. . . . It was appraised at $55,000."

"Is that right? Who did the appraisal for you?"

"A Realtor wanted to list it for us and did a free appraisal. He said it would easily sell for $55,000—maybe $55,500. We just want to sell it quickly because my husband was transferred."

"What do you need the $900 for?"

"Well, we figured it would help pay for the moving costs, and we wanted to get *something* out of it."

"Your ad said the house is one year old. Are you the first owners?"

"Yes, we are."

"How long have you had it for sale?"

"This is the first week."

"Where is it located?"

"The address is 2342 Hannon Street. Do you know where that is?"

"I sure do. . . . Can we set a time when I can take a look it?"

I'll let you in on my thoughts while I consider it.

Knowing the area, I can tell that it is in the right kind of neighborhood. The houses in that neighborhood are in good condition, and the whole area is blooming. The owners have no equity to speak of, so the house will be selling close to top dollar. The Realtor's appraisal is at best an educated guess, and many times a Realtor will puff up an appraisal to get the listing.

If I buy it as a rental property I couldn't get more than $500 a month in that area, which would mean a negative cash flow until the house was sold. But it's a small alligator, and I would recoup my losses with tax savings. Buying it with only

$900 down (and I might get them to take $500), and having that great FHA I can assume for $45 (the assumption fee charged by most lenders), I'll bet my total closing costs will be under $2,000. That's a small investment, and with it I'll be controlling over $50,000 worth of real estate.

I could buy it now and rent it for a year and my total investment will still be under $3,000. I will get all of that back in tax savings, and I know that with that area growing like it is the house should sell somewhere close to $55,000. If I can get them to sell it for $52,500, I'll make $2,500. Well, at least it's worth looking at.

That's how I find good deals in the paper. I read every word in the ad carefully, looking for clues. In that ad the words "no qualifying" told me it was probably a VA or FHA loan, and I was right. An assumable bank loan usually doesn't require that the new buyer qualify before assuming it.

Anything that isn't in the ad needs to be discussed. What is the sellers' motivation? What is the selling price? How did they arrive at that price? What is the balance of the loan? Is it assumable, and if it is, what is the interest rate and how much are the payments? Do the payments include taxes and insurance?

One of the most important questions is "How long has your house been for sale?" If a house has been for sale for some time, then obviously the owners aren't asking the market price or offering attractive terms. If you have already spent some time learning property values, you shouldn't have any difficulty spotting the problem and solving it. And time pressure is on your side.

Let's use a concrete example: There is a nice three-bedroom home in the neighborhood that has been for sale for three months. The owners are asking $75,000, and you know that the market price is right around $70,000. Worse than the price, however, is the terms. The owners have $22,000 equity in their home and they want all of it in cash. That means a trip to the bank and—if you can qualify—a high-interest loan.

If you weren't aware that the house had been for sale for some time, you might simply walk away. Knowing, however, that the owners are probably getting anxious by now, you find yourself in the driver's seat. The excitement of selling has long since lost its luster, and with every passing day they become more and more a "don't wanter."

If, after talking to the owners and finding out that they really only *need* $6,000 (to put on a house they want to buy), you present an offer of, say, $68,000, with $6,000 down and payments on the remainder at 10 percent, what are your chances of acceptance? Much, much better than they were three months ago. And, if your offer is rejected, how much better will your chances be three months from now?

One of the first questions I ask every time I pick up the phone to call a seller is "How long has your property been for sale?" You may not expect them to give you such vital information, but at least nine out of ten sellers will be happy to tell you. If it has been more than a couple of months, a red flag should go up and bells should clang. There is a problem and if you can find a solution you may have an excellent deal waiting.

A few of the most common reasons for a long selling period are:

1. The asking price is too high and the sellers are inflexible.
2. The sellers are not offering good terms (they want cash for their equity).
3. They have an incompetent agent, or none at all.
4. They don't really want to sell; they just want to find out what their house will sell for.

A student of mine told me about a classified ad he found one night that read, "Must sell this week. 2 bdrm 1 bath. 9% assumable mortgage, $39,000." The price was unbelievable for the area, so he called immediately.

The owner had listed the house with a Realtor, who assured him that the house would easily sell for $50,000. (My student said that he felt the house would never have sold for more than $45,000.) So the house was listed in April and the owner, strapped for cash, made a giant mistake: Trusting the Realtor to sell it quickly, he stopped making payments on the house.

Three months went by. The real estate agent's listing contract expired. And a very disgusted, anxious, and frightened man—who hadn't made a house payment in three months—placed an ad that looked to an investor like a K-Mart blue-light special. The hapless owner didn't want *anything* for his equity. The existing loan for $38,500 (at 9 percent) was fully assumable, and for the price of three back payments—totaling $960 cash—and the assumption of that gorgeous loan, the house was sold. Why? An incompetent real estate agent, a very tragic mistake on the part of the homeowner, and *time pressure.*

Making the Call

Remember that about half the ads will eliminate themselves. The prices will be too high, or they are obviously looking for the full market price. Most of the other half—the ones you do call on—will have one problem or another and will also be eliminated by your phone call. This sifting process is good; if you had to visit every house listed in the paper, your investing career would be short-lived.

To make calling easier, I've designed a checklist that you can fill out while you are talking to the owner. By using the checklist on every property, you can be sure you have all the information you need, and you can keep that information straight—it can get confusing after five or six calls.

By asking the right questions you can make your phone calling a highly efficient investing tool. Don't be afraid to ask why the owners need the cash, or what they intend to do with it. This is vital information to you, as it will help you determine their needs and assist you in making an acceptable offer. Besides, I've had several sellers respond with, "Well, I don't really *need* the money at all. . . . I just figured I'd buy this and that and put the rest in the bank." An answer like that is all you need to suggest they lend you the money—on a seller-financed contract.

TELEPHONE CHECKLIST

Telephone(s): _____ Date _____

Description: _____

Address: _____ City _____

Owner's Name(s): _____

Asking Price: _____

How was price arrived at: _____

How long for sale: _____

Property Description:

Age of house: _____

# of bedrooms: _____ Baths: _____

Other rooms: _____

_____

Garage: _____ Lot size and shape: _____

Other features: _____

Loan Information:

1st Mortgage:

    mortgagee (lender) _____

    assumable? _____ interest rate _____

    approx. loan balance _____ payment _____

    Is the rate fixed, or will it increase? _____

      Increase to what rate? _____

      What will the new payments be? _____

Does the monthly payment include taxes and insurance? _____

If not, how much are taxes and insurance? _____

2nd Mortgage:

mortgagee (lender) _____

assumable? _____ interest rate _____

approx. loan balance _____ payment _____

Is the rate fixed, or will it increase? _____

Increase to what rate? _____

What will the new payments be? _____

Total Balance _____ Total Payment _____

Asking Price _____

— Total Balance _____

= Owner's Equity _____

How is the seller's equity to be paid? _____

Will owner give financing? _____

Owner's *need* for cash _____

Lowest price considered _____

Comments: _____

_____

_____

_____

Decision:

_____ See property: Date _____   Time _____

_____ Keep on file for follow-up

2. Classified Ads #2: Placing an Ad

This is the other side of the same coin, but *you* will be the one doing the advertising. Place an ad in the same paper, or in what I call the "fish wrapper" paper—the throw-away paper that comes in the mail once a week, with nothing but advertising, that most people toss out without reading. I place an ad every week that says,

> I buy homes. Call or write Steve Wayner at (305)255-0601 P.O. Box 562047 Miami, Fla. 33256.

The ad costs me $39 a week, and every week I get between ten and twenty responses. If I only find two good deals a year with this ad, I will be well rewarded for my effort. (I find at least five or six such deals every year with this method.) Placing such an ad is a "shotgun" approach to investing, as is the next.

3. Door Knockers

The door knocker is a flyer I have had printed that says, "I buy houses." It explains that I am interested in hearing from home owners if they are planning on selling their homes. I send out a thousand flyers, at a cost of about $40, and I pay local teenagers to distribute them to every home in my area.

Most people will glance at the flyer once and throw it away, but at least a handful will either call right away or keep the flyer for the future. Six months down the road you may get a phone call and have that exceptional deal find you.

The last time I used this method of advertising I hired four high school students, who spent six hours distributing five-hundred door knockers. My total cost was $200, and I bought two homes as a result, making this one of the most profitable investments I've ever made.

In the last two methods for finding good deals, you should take note that their biggest advantage is that the owners are calling you, not vice versa. You don't have to make one phone call, and the owners are not going to call you unless they are already interested in selling. They are much more likely to be anxious "don't wanters."

4. Bird Dogs

If you don't have the time to be calling and driving, someone else surely does. The term "bird dog" is often used to describe a person who has the time to find deals but not the money to buy. For a flat fee—or a commission—your bird dogs will do your bargain hunting for you.

Who would make the best bird dogs? Well, it should be someone who gets around, who sees the neighborhoods in your area, and who is likely to notice when a house goes up for sale or suddenly becomes vacant. What about the mailman? Or the paper boy? They both spend time going from door to door, and they would be apt to notice what's going on in the neighborhood. What paper boy wouldn't be happy to let you know that the Wilsons on Sycamore are moving . . . especially if he will make $200 if you actually buy the house?

Check with clergymen in the area. When people are moving into or out of an area, the clergy are often the first to know. And when people are in financial trouble, the rabbi or pastor often gets the first phone call. You are providing a helpful service; you are a professional problem solver, and you can be proud of it.

Large businesses in the area will often have employees transferred in or out. They could use a name and phone number to refer to their employees. And what does it cost you? Only a small initial investment of time and no money at all.

Another time-saver is a business card that says, "I buy houses, call me." Attach the card to every bill you pay; pin one on every bulletin board in every laundromat and grocery store in your city. The time and money invested is minimal, and the rewards can be great.

People are not going to know that you want to buy houses until you tell them. There is no magical mental telepathy that will suddenly inform everyone in the state that you are going to invest in real estate. Everyone you know and everyone you meet is a potential ally—if you will let them help.

5. Real Estate Agents

Many investors feel some hesitancy about working with Realtors, and their fears are not completely groundless. Too many Realtors don't understand investors; they are trained to work with home buyers, and they are entirely unaware of the potential that exists in working with an investor. Considering the money-making power of real estate, it's hard to believe that every Realtor isn't investing full time. But the truth is that many Realtors have no interest in investing. They are like a blind man in a speedboat, rowing because they don't realize it is equipped with a built-in engine.

Because of their lack of investing desire, it isn't hard to find Realtors who are willing to help. After all, they certainly aren't any competition. Try this: Walk into a realty office and approach a Realtor. Ask, "Do you know what an investor looks like?" The usual response is "No." Point to yourself. Then tell the Realtor exactly what you are looking for. In most cases they will be very helpful.

One Realtor was able to show me forty-seven REOs (Real Estate Owned, the name given to properties taken back by the lender in a foreclosure. Most banks and savings and loans have a few REOs on their books, and these properties are a liability to the bank.) I made an offer on six of them, and as of the writing of this book, it looks as though I will get four of them.

Don't ignore Realtors as a source of good deals. In the next chapter I'll give you a few more pointers on how to add a good real estate agent to your investment team—and one good agent is worth his or her weight in gold.

6. "For Sale" Signs

One thing you should be doing by now is driving through your selected areas at least once a week. When a house in the area goes up for sale, the owners or their agent will usually hammer a large sign into the lawn with giant letters that say FOR SALE. What more do you need? It's unlikely they will be mailing out engraved invitations, so you should definitely take them up on their public notice.

Stop by and talk to the owners. They will often be happy to let you walk through and take a closer look at their home. Look at the home not only through the eyes of a potential buyer, but also as a seller. If you do buy the house, you'll undoubtedly be selling it later. What changes will you have to make, and how much will they cost? Now is the time to begin making up your long-range plan.

If the house is for sale through an agent, you may have to call the agent and make an appointment to see the house. When you call the agent, find out as much as you can over the phone about the price and terms. If it sounds like a possible good deal, contact your own friendly agent and have him or her look into the details for you.

7. Fixers

The ugly duckling has made more money for more investors than any other classification of real estate. You've no doubt seen this brand of house: mud-spattered walls, peeling paint, one screen torn halfway off, weeds (the few that aren't dead) sprawling across the driveway, and maybe one or two broken windows for good measure. If you've thought anything at all, it was probably, "Well, *somebody* doesn't care much for this house. What an eyesore!"

The time has come to change your way of looking and thinking. A smart real estate investor would drive by the same property and think, "You know, I bet it wouldn't take more than a week and a couple hundred dollars to get that thing into shape. . . . I wonder what they want for it." Owners with little pride in their homes will often be ready to sell and happy to walk away from at least part of their potential equity in exchange for getting out without having to clean up.

I do know a few investors who can't be bothered fixing up houses. They prefer to wait for the occasional "don't wanters" who happen to have nice, clean homes for sale. The fact is, however, that the houses you'll find selling below their market value are usually owned by people in trouble. Unless they are suddenly forced to move because of a transfer, the trouble has existed for some time. In those situations it is not out of the ordinary for the house to have been neglected for some time.

The price of a house and its general condition are closely related, of course. Most prospective buyers are looking for a place to live, and they are repelled by overgrown lawns and dirty carpets. They know that they could fix the place up themselves, but they are really looking for something nicer . . . something that looks more like home. So the seller is forced to clean up the house and try again or *lower the price*.

As an investor you should be looking for houses that need minor repairs. If you've been studying home values for a while and know that every house on Elm Street is selling for $65,000 to $70,000, you won't be surprised when the little brown one at 2314 East Elm appears on the market selling for $60,000. The yard has been neglected for some time (the first sign of a "don't wanter") and you've been keeping your eye on it. Fixed up, it would sell for $66,000 or so, but the way it looks now nobody would pay more than $57,000 to live there. You have no intention of living there. You offer $57,000 and settle at $58,500.

If the house looks empty you may be onto a real deal. Leave a note on the door, announcing yourself as an interested buyer, and write a letter to the owners at the address of the house. If they have left a forwarding address, it will reach them. *Someone* is making payments on the property, and that someone will be happy to hear from you.

We'll cover the specifics of fixing up homes later in the book. For now, keep them in mind as a possible source of good deals.

8. Foreclosure Sales

This is really an area for more experienced investors, but I have had students who insisted on getting their feet wet by jumping headfirst into foreclosure sales. Most of them survived the dunking.

Whenever a foreclosure is to take place, the lender will publish a notice before the day of the auction, letting the public know about it. These "Notices of Sale" must be published a month or so before the sale, and they must be published where the public can read them. In many smaller communities such notices are published in the daily paper, usually right before the classified ads. In larger cities, however, they may only be published in a legal journal.

Ordinarily it's better to contact the owners before the auction and work out a deal. You'll have more chance of getting the terms you want, and you can avoid the auction requirements of an all-cash bid.

Any owners who are facing foreclosure are obvious candidates for "Don't Wanter of the Month Club." The legal notice will give you the address of the property. Then it is up to you; you may wish to knock on the door, give them your business card, and explain that you would be interested in buying their home, or you may send them a letter that does the same and invites inquiries. Tact is the byword in dealing with such owners. They are more often than not at least a little sensitive—if not downright angry—and may not want to discuss it. They are definite "don't wanters" of the first rank, but they may be unwilling to work with you. Then it's on to the sale.

Mortgages that have been defaulted on may or may not include a **power of sale.** Without the power of sale, the foreclosed property is sold in court, and the owner has (in some states) up to eighteen months to redeem the property. Mortgages with a power of sale can be sold like trust deeds—at public auction. The sale of a defaulted trust deed is technically a **trustee's sale,** rather than a foreclosure, but the effect is the same, so I will use the more familiar term of foreclosure.

Each state has its own laws that govern these sales, so I recommend you check with a real estate attorney in your state before getting involved with foreclosure sales.

The legal notice will include the time and place of the sale. But before you show up at the auction with checkbook in hand, you'll need to learn all you can about the property. You will want to inspect it, determine its value, and search the title for any nasty surprises such as tax liens. We'll discuss inspections and title searches in more depth in the last section of the book.

At the auction the party owed the money will usually start the bidding with the amount needed to satisfy the debt, make any delinquent payments, and cover any legal fees involved. If there is any equity beyond that, the ranks of investors step in and begin bidding for the property. If, for example, a house was worth $80,000, and the total amount needed to satisfy the loan was $60,000, there would be $20,000 equity available for the investors to fight over. If nobody else showed up except yourself, you could bid $60,001 and walk away with the deal of the year. But that will rarely be the case. In most instances the bank will make the only bid and that will be the end of it, since foreclosures usually happen in cases where properties are overburdened with debt and there is little or no equity.

Another difficulty encountered will be the fact that the buyer at auction is often required to pay the entire price in cash (or a cashier's check). Therefore, the game calls for players with a *lot* of extra money on their hands.

If you are still interested in foreclosure auctions, by all means give them a try. If you have the time and money to pursue them, they can be the best source of high profits in real estate. I know a few investors who do nothing but haunt foreclosure sales with cashier's checks in hand. They find the occasional deal like the one in the example above, and make $10,000 to $20,000 or more at a time.

"Don't Wanters"

Anyone who doesn't want his or her property for one more day is a possible source of good deals. Unfortunately, many people who are true don't wanters are such because of one tragedy or another: a lost job, a death, a divorce, a transfer, etc. Keep in mind that you, as an investor, are able to solve what is usually a terrifying problem that is threatening to tear them apart. Don't ever allow anyone to convince you that investors are vultures feeding off the misfortunes of others. Without you there to buy that house, what would the sellers do? Probably lose the property. Probably watch the bank take over the house, kick them out, and destroy their credit. You aren't responsible for their misfortune, but you can solve their problem. *Become a problem solver.*

Eight methods of finding good deals are more than enough to get you started. If you've already been spending time looking in your investing area, and you're using these methods, it won't be long before you find your first deal. But beware! There are pitfalls waiting for you, and an investing mistake can cost you thousands of dollars. Therefore, take heed of

The Seven Warnings

1. Never fall in love with a property.

This somewhat cryptic advice means simply that you should never put yourself in a position where it is obvious to the other party that you are eager to buy (or sell).

It is a standard rule of good negotiators always to be willing to walk away from the table. As long as your attitude is obviously "this deal isn't going to make or break me," the other person is always trying to convince you that the transaction is in your best interest. But the minute you let even a hint of "I just have to have this property" show on your face, you might as well stop negotiating right there and sign on the dotted line.

Roger Dawson tells of a house that he was looking at as a possible residence. He is a nationally acclaimed negotiations expert, so he knew he would have little difficulty getting the best price possible. He talked to the owners nonchalantly, walking away from the house calmly but excited inside. The price was fair—and would get much better before he was through—and the home was beautiful. He told his family about it and his wife and daughter immediately stopped by to take a peek. They walked through oohing and ahhing, and by the end of the tour it was obvious that if Roger ever wanted to enjoy a happy home again he would have to buy the house—at any price.

Don't fall in love with *any* property. Always be a "don't wanter." If you find yourself thinking that you just can't live without it, you probably can and should—especially when it comes to investment property.

2. Don't waste your time with inflexible sellers.

This is a common mistake made by new investors, especially those inclined to disregard the first warning. There are always other deals.

Of the thousands of sellers who advertise their homes every day, only a very, very few of them are really motivated to sell. The rest want to sell, but they are unwilling—or unable—to lower the price or offer better terms. Only 10 percent of all sellers are truly motivated to sell; the other 90 percent really aren't worth wasting your time on. That means you may have to make ten calls to find the one seller who will talk terms.

It's important to realize that flexibility means more than a willingness to lower the price or the down payment. The sellers may insist on a 10 percent down payment, but may be willing to accept it in four annual payments. Or, instead of lowering the price, they may be willing to raise the price, lower the down payment, and take payments on their equity at a low interest rate. An extremely flexible or inflexible seller is rare; almost every seller falls somewhere between the two extremes.

Whenever you call a seller, try to first determine why he or she is selling. That will be your first clue as to flexibility. Then ask, "Are you willing to be flexible on the price or the terms?" If there is little chance of concessions, thank the seller politely and hang up; no sense wasting your time with someone who doesn't really want to sell.

3. Don't over-improve a property.

If you want to add a swimming pool and an indoor jacuzzi, go right ahead—if it's your own residence. In investment property, however, improvements will rarely increase the value of the property more than the cost involved. A commandment of investing is "Thou shalt not improve the property unless it will magnify thy rental income accordingly." Having the best house on the block will give you a nice warm feeling, but overimprovement is generally a waste of time and money.

As a guideline, the ideal situation is to buy the worst house in a nice neighborhood and then fix it up until it is above average. The reason is simple: When you first start fixing up, every dollar invested will return a hundred. Simply mowing the lawn and watering the rose bushes can bring a price increase of a thousand dollars. But as the condition—and therefore the market value—of the house begins to approach that of the general neighborhood, further improvements won't make much difference in the market value.

If it is to be a rental property, why not get the tenants to make the improvements at their own expense? All you need to do is give your permission for the improvements and make sure the lease agreement specifies that improvements will stay with the property. Many tenants take pride in their homes and will fix them up for you.

4. Don't do all the work yourself.
You can do anything you want, of course, but I usually recommend using experts, especially if the improvements called for are more extensive than repainting the trim. Too many investors start out with the "I want to do it myself" attitude, trying to squeeze every last penny out of the deal. Most of the time they are throwing away dollars to save a few pennies.

A friend of mine thought he was a real handyman—right up until he made his $15,000 mistake. He wanted to add a bathroom to his property, and he estimated that by doing it himself he would pay only $3,400, saving over a thousand dollars that he would otherwise have to pay to a professional. What he didn't consider was the city building codes. His improvements failed to meet the minimum standards, and upgrading the electrical and plumbing systems brought his total bill up to $15,000—a far cry from $3,400.

Remember that experts are charging you extra for their *expertise* that has been earned through years of experience. The old saying is still true: If something is worth doing, it's worth doing right.

5. Don't mistake a national disaster for a "fixer-upper."
When I recommend buying houses that need a little fixing up, I don't mean houses with "Condemned" signs hanging all over them. There are a few danger signals that will clue you in to

those properties that will require a fix-up budget the size of the national debt.

Don't buy a fixer-upper if the fixing up includes reroofing the entire house and rebuilding the basement. Those repairs will cost a fortune and you may never recover their cost in the sale. I'm not saying there isn't money in major restoration, but if you're just getting started you'll find it's easier to stick to minor repair work.

Don't take on plumbing or electrical repairs or any other projects that require an experienced hand unless that hand is at the end of your arm. Call in an expert when an expert is needed, and if you can see that such repairs will be needed, get an estimate *before* you buy the house and have the seller give you a credit at closing for the repairs.

Do buy property if all the needed repairs are cosmetic, such as a dying lawn, overgrown weeds, trash in the yard, crayon marks on the walls, torn wallpaper, and dirty carpets. Every one of these can be taken care of quickly, with a minimum of expense, and they will increase the selling price dramatically.

6. Don't invest before you're ready.
I get calls from students who, in their haste to get started, have managed to tie themselves into a losing deal and who suddenly expect me to untie them. A contract is binding; *don't* start making offers before you've thoroughly analyzed an investment.

Later in the book I'll be helping you write offers that include what I call "success clauses." These clauses will allow you to control your offer and, if necessary, back out of the deal before closing unscathed.

Here are the steps you should go through before making your first offer:

1. **Learn Values.** Look at houses for sale; get to know selling prices; talk to sellers, agents, and other experts. Reach a point where you feel comfortable estimating market values.

2. **Assemble a Team.** In the next chapter you'll meet your investing team; a team of experts who'll help

you with every step of every investment. Without your team you're working alone . . . and that's a good way to get into trouble.

3. **Analyze a Potential Deal Thoroughly.** As we go along through this book, I'll continue to teach you how to analyze an investment. When you've done a thorough analysis of market value, repair estimations, and profit projections, *then* you'll be ready to make an offer.

7. Don't buy alligators.

There was a time, not long ago, when it made sense to buy alligators (negative cash flow properties). After all, if you could feed them out of your own pocket for a year or so, they would certainly appreciate more than enough to cover your expenses.

If you've analyzed an investment and you're *positive* you will recoup your out-of-pocket expenses, then you might consider buying a nasty pet. But when you're just getting started, you're much better off waiting for the exceptional deal—the one where the owners are willing to give up substantial equity in exchange for a quick sale.

You can find seminars and books all over the country where you will learn how to buy real estate with nothing down. That's not the hard part; the hard part is finding positive cash flow.

There are sleepers and keepers. If you have a property with negative cash flow in your portfolio, you've been asleep on the job. That alligator is sitting there eating you up alive! Get rid of it and look for keepers—properties that are worth keeping because they are making money every month. You should try to find at least a couple of keepers every year. The build-up of equity and increases in rental income will create a retirement income that will beat the socks off Social Security and pension plans.

In Chapter Seven we'll take another look at negative cash flow, and I'll give you at least one good strategy for eliminating your alligators. For now, however, keep in mind that it's not the investor who buys the first property who wins; it's the one who buys the *best* investment. Take your time; throw the little deals back in the water and wait for the truly exceptional ones.

Do It Right

Every one of the warnings above are based on common sense. And every one of them has been ignored by at least one eager would-be investor. Taking heed of every one of the warnings won't guarantee success; neither will using every one of the eight methods for finding good deals. It will take all of that and more. It will take determination, patience, and a strong unwillingness to quit. Give yourself at least six months of hard work and unending study before you evaluate your progress. And obey

The Six Commandments

These "commandments" are more than investing tips; they are the rules by which every successful person guides his or her life. Whether or not you become a real estate investor, if you'll incorporate all six into your life you *will* succeed.

1. Have a Game Plan.
I graduated very high in my law school class. I wasn't the smartest person; I know for a fact there were much smarter students. And yet I graduated near the top. Why? Because I had a game plan.

Every Saturday I wrote a complete outline of the course material covered. Sometimes it took me two hours, sometimes as long as eight, but I completed the outline every week without fail. By the time final exams came up, I had two hundred to three hundred pages completed. One week before exams I would pare that down to a fifty-page outline, and three days before I would condense that to only four pages of key words. I'd then spend the last three days memorizing those four pages, and on exam day it was easy to write those four pages from memory. With those key words in hand, I literally had an entire course outline to work from. *Then* I would look at the exam questions. With an outline in front of me, answering the questions was simple.

I succeeded as a law student because I had a game plan. I had worked out a system that was unbeatable, and I used that system religiously. The same is true for any endeavor; plan for your success, don't just wait for it to happen. You can make up your own game plan by obeying commandment two:

2. Set Goals.

You've already heard the same advice time and time again, but have you followed it yet? Have you set long- and short-range goals for your success? In this section I'm going to help you make up your own goals—achievable goals—based on your own personal desires. Setting goals and then following through is easy—if you use common sense.

Step 1: How wealthy do you want to be in five years, and then in ten years? Set a dollar amount and *write it down*.

Step 2: How many houses must you buy and sell or buy and rent to achieve your five-year and ten-year goals? This will be more difficult to ascertain until you've had some hands-on experience, but you can estimate and revise those estimates as you gain experience.

Step 3: How much time will it take each week to achieve your goals? You'll have to budget your time to find the extra hours. Example:

    A. Fifteen hours per week
       1. two hours per day (five days a week) calling, talking to sellers.
       2. five hours every Saturday driving, looking at houses, following up on possible deals.

B. Break down weekly goals into daily
tasks. I recommend using a daily planner
and writing down a definite daily schedule. List exactly how your time will be
spent:
1. calling sellers
2. looking at houses
3. reading MLS books
4. attending investment group meetings
5. reading investment books

If you start with long-range plans and work your way
backward to daily assignments, you can only succeed. However, following a strict schedule is tough, which is why you
should also follow the next commandment:

3. Reward Thyself.
Rewarding yourself for your successes isn't tough; it's just tough
to do it right. When you take that first check to the bank for
$3,000, you may be tempted to reward yourself with a Euro-
pean vacation. Resist! Spend $300—or maybe $500—on yourself and reinvest the balance. The magic of investing is that you
can not only add to your success; you can multiply it! A thousand dollars spent today is only a thousand, while a thousand
invested today may mean ten thousand next year.

If you spend all your profits, you'll still be struggling ten
years from now to get ahead. You'll still have to depend on
every deal to keep you going. Granted, you'll have a nice stereo
system and maybe even a couple of sporty cars. But if you can
force yourself to reinvest most of your profit, ten years from
now your money will have doubled, tripled, or multiplied itself
ten times.

Don't fail to reward yourself either. If you insist on playing Midas, loving your profit for its own sake and reinvesting
every penny, you'll soon find yourself completely burned out,
used up, wasted. Those rewards are what make investing fun;
they make all the work worthwhile.

4. Be Fair.

A few years ago I read an article in the newspaper that I've never forgotten. A paper boy, only fourteen years old, had befriended one of his customers, an elderly woman who lived alone in a tiny, run-down house. He started helping her with her yard work, and then, as he spent more and more time with her, he found out she was eating TV dinners. She would thaw them out on the kitchen counter and eat them at room temperature—her oven hadn't worked for a couple of years. He figured out how to fix the oven, and from that day on he and the woman were practically inseparable until the day of her death.

When her affairs were settled it was discovered that she had left her estate to her paper boy—the entire 2.2 million dollars.

In your dealings with sellers, you will often be working with a "don't wanter"—someone in trouble. It's easy to take advantage of such a person, and that's exactly how real estate investors have earned a bad name for themselves. If you're a problem solver, instead of a problem, you'll not only have the gratitude of the hapless seller, you'll also sleep better at night. Not only that, you'll also be establishing a reputation.

I recently got an excellent deal because I had treated a seller well. She told a neighbor that I had helped her with her problem and that I had treated her fairly. The neighbor also wanted to sell, so guess who he called first? That's right; he called me and offered to sell me his house. The terms and price were excellent, and it was the easiest deal of my life—and all because I was willing to solve someone's problem instead of taking advantage of it.

The golden rule—do unto others as you would have them do unto you—has been around for a while. Why? Because you are always rewarded. I know it works because I've used it, and I know many investors who've done the same. In negotiating we call it the Win/Win principle. If you make the sellers feel that you are aware of and sympathetic to their situation, they will do everything they can to be fair; if you act as though you have them over a barrel, they will do everything they can to resist you.

Go out of your way to help your sellers . . . You just never know what your reward will be.

5. Do It Now.

Tomorrow is too late. Action is the key to success. If you put this book down and say, "Interesting ideas; I'll have to try them out some time," you might as well give up right now. I can't stress this point enough, and you'll hear it again as we go along. As I've watched thousands of people attend seminars and get excited about investing, it's struck me again and again that the difference between the 90 percent who'll never do anything and the 10 percent who will succeed is that the 10 percent will *do something* more than think about it.

Do you wish you had started investing in real estate in the mid-'70s? If you do, what do you think you will be wishing in the year 2000, when you look back over the '80s and '90's? If you've spent that time waiting for the perfect moment, you won't be any further ahead, will you? Common sense strikes again. *If you do nothing, nothing will happen.*

6. Never Give Up.

Common sense again: Those who give up can't possibly succeed, and those who refuse to give up can't possibly fail. Take Walter, for example. His father discouraged his attempts to succeed at every turn. Leaving home, he started his own company at eighteen. Within a few years he had built up a decent business, only to have his business partner stolen away from him by an unscrupulous businessman. Refusing to give up, he moved across the country and started again. After rebuilding his business he again had his best and brightest helpers seduced away by a competitor. Unstoppable, he rebuilt to the point where his company was recognized across the country. And even then his father remained unconvinced. When Walter bought a large building for his growing company and took his father on a tour of the property, his comment was "What will you do with the building?" What he meant was "What will you do with the building when your business fails?" Walter, thinking quickly, reassured his father that it could be turned into a hospital. The response mollified his father's worries, but once again Walter had been slapped in the face by the one he most wanted to impress. He certainly could have quit at any point, and many others would have. But not Walter; he never, ever gave up.

And today we can enjoy a day at Disneyland, the creation of Walter E. Disney, a man absolutely unwilling to give up.

You *can* achieve almost anything . . . if you persevere.

Sometimes I hear the complaint that real estate is boring. I'll concede the point. Buying and selling houses can be a slow, messy business. For fun it just can't compare with trading silver futures or buying the latest high-tech stock. And, because real estate investing isn't much fun, many new investors quit before they ever make a dime for their efforts. But it's funny what $8,000 in cash can do for perspective, however. Success is sweet, and one taste is usually enough to instill a craving for more.

Do you work for a living now? Do you enjoy your work? If you are a member of the majority, you go to work forty hours or more each week and resent every minute of it. You hate the alarm clock; you feel trapped, chained to your desk. And yet you intend to do the same thing forty hours every week until you retire. Yes; reading real estate books can be tiring, and a long day at work doesn't leave much enthusiasm for calling sellers every night for an hour. Of course Saturday is your day off, and driving around the neighborhood talking to owners isn't a real hoot. So what? If you can force yourself to endure the tedium inherent in educating yourself, you will be starting a new life.

I'm not selling a pipe dream here, my friend. Your success isn't waiting around the corner with a club, hoping you'll show up so you can be crowned with glory. If you want to see your dreams fulfilled, you're going to have to *work*. There isn't any other way.

I feel myself pushing against a wall when I talk to most people about investing. The wall is made from a thousand bricks, and each one is stamped "I can't." After spending a lifetime building the wall, few can see over it. They hear my voice on the other side saying, "Yes, you can!" but they just shake their heads and turn away. I run out of encouraging words after a while, and I've learned that it's impossible for me to tear down somebody else's wall.

Set some goals; dream your dreams; and put yourself through the toughest year of your life. Sacrifice a few precious sessions in front of the tube and invest your future. And I promise you that all the hours of boredom will be well paid the first time you sell a property and put five or ten thousand dollars in the bank.

And above all else, DON'T QUIT!

The philosophy "I think I can, I think I can . . ." is always rewarded by "I did it, I did it. . . ."

Record Keeping

This should maybe be the seventh commandment: Keep good records. Accurate record keeping is perhaps the most important difference between a successful investor and the investor who is always wondering where the money went.

Do you own a filing cabinet yet? If not, you are probably using the shoe box method for filing your receipts. Get a filing cabinet before you even think of buying real estate! Every property must have its own file or set of files. I label those files with a two-number system that accounts for the year of the purchase and the address of the property. If I bought a house at 12445 S.W. 165 Street in 1984, I would label that file 84-12445. By doing so, and by keeping my files in numerical order, they are automatically sorted according to year and are easy to find. Also, I don't have to worry about duplicate names.

What should you put into the files? *Everything* that relates to the property. I suggest buying the dividers that hold several folders each. Label the divider with the property code, and for each property have a set of folders. There should be a folder for purchasing information, management information, and selling information. Beyond that, you can make your own system as extensive as you wish.

You may wish to make up your own standard forms, or you may purchase forms that are available in stationery and office supply stores. A typewriter and a copy machine are sufficient for making a highly efficient filing system.

Here are a few of the many things you will want to include in your filing:

- The name(s) of the sellers and their current address and telephone number.
- The attorney who represented the sellers (name and phone number).
- The attorney who represented you (name and phone number).
- The name, address, and phone number of the mortgage lender, loan number, and the amount of the payments.
- The name, address, and phone number of the insurance company.
- A brief description of the coverage and a copy of the policy.
- Neighborhood schools: names, addresses, and phone numbers.
- Name, address, and phone number of real estate agent(s) involved.
- Inspections (name, address, phone number, inspection date, and copies of inspection reports):
  - Termite
  - Roof
  - Pool
  - etc.
- Every utility company that services the property: names, addresses, and phone numbers.

These are a few important items, along with copies of every important document that relates to the sale. For property management, you will want to keep copies of all rental applications and agreements, all expenses and receipts, and all correspondence (including written transcripts of verbal exchanges) with the tenants. If you aren't sure whether you should save a document, by all means *do* . . . it can't hurt. And if it doesn't seem to fit into any file, make a new file for it.

I can't stress enough how easy a decent filing system— or how miserable a poor one—will make your life. Start your record keeping system today, and if it doesn't work perfectly for you, refine it as you go along.

Chapter Three Summary

I. You must have at least one workable method for finding good deals; they won't come looking for you. The following eight methods have been used by enough investors to prove their worth:
   1. Classified ads—calling sellers.
   2. Classified ads—placing an "I buy houses" ad.
   3. Door knockers—distributing flyers.
   4. Bird dogs—if you don't have the time, someone else does.
   5. Realtors—they have the resources for locating deals.
   6. "For Sale" signs—drive around and keep your eyes open.
   7. Fixers—those run-down houses may be gold mines in disguise.
   8. Foreclosures—either before or at the auction, an excellent source of "don't wanters."

II. Once you've found a possible deal, watch out for these pitfalls:
   1. Never fall in love with a property. If you feel that you can't live without it, you should probably run away from it as fast as you can.
   2. Don't waste your time with inflexible sellers. A truly motivated seller will be willing to negotiate.
   3. Don't over-improve a property. Fixing up a property is great—to a point. Keep an eye on

ROI— Return On Investment. Some minor fix-up will more than pay for itself; beyond that, you're probably throwing your money away.

4. Don't do all the work yourself. It takes a team of experts to put together a good deal. Don't think you have to do everything yourself: You'll be wasting your time, your money, and your labor.

5. Don't mistake a national disaster for a "fixer-upper." Major repairs are often surprisingly expensive. If your cursory inspection doesn't reveal anything major but a more careful scrutiny later does, you can always back out then.

6. Don't invest before you're ready. How long have you waited so far? Ten, twenty years? You can wait another three months (or however long it takes to learn the basics). Your first transaction should be one of your best; you can't afford many mistakes when you're dealing in the tens of thousands of dollars.

7. Don't buy alligators. Stick with the positive cash flows, and leave the negative for other investors who think all the money is at the end of a long, thin branch. Don't inherit someone else's problems and think it makes you a shrewd investor.

III. If your goal is true success and a life filled with achievement, follow these six commandments:

1. Have a game plan. Create your own workable system and stay with it, rather than using a haphazard approach.

2. Set goals. Set long-range goals first and work your way backward to daily plans of action. The people who get furthest in life are those who know where they are, where they're going, and how they're going to get there.

3. Reward thyself. Don't get mired in the daily struggle for wealth; take time to pat yourself on the back occasionally. But don't go overboard,

either. Reinvest at least 90 percent of your profits and watch them multiply.

4. Be fair. I know how easy it is to take advantage of someone in trouble: I've been there myself. But experience has shown that taking the longer route and going out of your way to be fair will always pay higher dividends in the end.

5. Do it now. Today isn't just the first day of the rest of your life; it's the only day you have available to prepare for tomorrow. You are where you are today as a result of how you've spent all of your previous todays.

6. Never give up. I can't recall the life story of any famous and successful person that wasn't filled with setbacks. Within the ranks of successful people, Walt Disney wasn't an exception; he simply shared with them that rare quality of unending persistence.

IV. Keep accurate records. Set up a property record-keeping system, now, *before* you have trouble.

Chapter Three Homework

1. Using the phone check list presented in this chapter, call at least five sellers tonight and every night this week. If any of them sound promising, set up an appointment to look at the house.

2. Either place an ad in a local paper or create a flyer of your own that says ''I buy houses'' and distribute it throughout your selected area.

3. Buy a daily planner and put it to use *now*. Set your long-range, mid-range, and short-range goals; plan a daily schedule and stick with it for at least one month.

4. Start a record-keeping system like the one described in this chapter, or devise a sysem of your own.

Part Two

Getting the Information

Chapter Four

You're Not Alone

Let's face it, if you're thinking about investing in real estate for the first time, you're talking about a very big undertaking. *Nobody* knows everything about real estate—and that's coming from a real estate attorney and a full-time investor and national lecturer. I don't pretend for a minute to know everything; that's why I continue to educate myself, and that's why I surround myself with an excellent team of experts.

In this chapter you'll meet some of those experts. We'll talk about how you can get their help—often for free—and how you can locate other sources of education to help you get started and keep going.

Education and Experience

Most of the trick to successful investing is experience. For me, after countless transactions, buying real estate isn't much more difficult than running to the store for a gallon of milk. I can do it because I've spent years gaining my education;

I've spent years gaining practical experience—making enough mistakes along the way to learn just about everything that can go wrong; and I've put together an excellent team of real estate experts to help me.

I've claimed that buying real estate isn't much more difficult for me than buying milk. But think about it for a minute. There is nothing particularly simple about driving to the store and buying milk. To drive, you must know how to start the car, how to operate the gears, the gas pedal, and the brake. You must know exactly where the store is and how to get there, and you must know the traffic laws in your own state. Once you get to the store safely, you must know how to locate the milk, how to tell if it's fresh, and you need to know if the price is right. Then it's up to the cash register, where you must deal with a clerk, watching his or her actions carefully to make sure you aren't overcharged. Back to the car, and repeat the driving lesson until you are safely home again.

You and I can go to the store without a thought, despite its complexity. Why? Because we have combined education and experience, the two most powerful tools that we humans have for growth and development. This book, and others like it, can provide you with that education. Professionals in your own city can act as your own personal tutors, and they are only a phone call away. Seminars, conventions, and workshops are taught every week all across the country. The educational resources are there; it is up to you to take advantage of them.

How many hours do you spend each day trying to improve your knowledge? If you spend less than ten hours every week learning, don't try to tell me you're serious about wanting to succeed. The knowledge will come with time and study. The amount of time depends on the quality of the study.

You feel afraid and inadequate now only because of your lack of knowledge. So what? Try asking a six-year-old to drive to the store and pick up a gallon of milk. Ridiculous? And yet in a few short years that child will be able to do it without even thinking about it. Give yourself some time, and get serious about your education.

I strongly recommend that you read at least one book

every month that teaches you something about investing. Also, if possible, you should attend at least one convention or seminar every couple of months. If you've missed a chance to hear a live seminar, don't pass up the next one. They are a great reminder when you think you're the only one in the world who is trying to invest. At these seminars you will meet hundreds of people just like you, and you will always go home refreshed, ready to tackle the world.

One of the best sources of new, up-to-date information is your newspaper. If you don't subscribe yet, call today. Not only do you need the classified section for calling sellers and looking up foreclosure information, but nearly every paper has a real estate section. The two local newspapers in my area, *The Miami News* and *The Miami Herald,* have fantastic business sections that are filled with information on current interest rates, economic cycles, and other news that will affect my investing. In the real estate section you will learn new tools for buying and selling. Every Sunday, *The Miami Herald* has a wonderful real estate section that always includes a column by a nationally syndicated writer, such as Robert Bruss, Lew Sichelman, or Kenneth R. Harney. Find out what day of the week your paper runs a real estate section (Sunday is the most common day). Most newspapers have real estate editors, and I've found that across the country these professionals have a wealth of knowledge to offer their readers. Don't forget about magazines such as *Money, Personal Finance, Changing Times, Home, Forbes,* and others which also supply up to date investment information.

You will only succeed if you *combine education with experience.* Don't try to invest without learning the basics first, and don't concentrate so hard on your education that you never do anything. A good combination of education and persistent effort will always be rewarded with success.

Meet the Experts

The following experts will help you at every stage of your real estate investing. Each one has spent years gaining his or her expertise, and they are waiting for someone like you to take advantage of it. In many cases you won't even have to pay for their help; they'll be happy to give you a hand in exchange for future profits.

Few people need to be convinced that buying a home is a complicated business. Imagine trying to buy Fred's house down the street without the help of professionals. Who would make sure all the paperwork necessary to prove the transfer of title was taken care of? Most buyers and sellers would be hopelessly lost trying to get together and agree on terms and trying to consummate a legally binding agreement.

Imagine the conversation:

"Okay, then, it's settled. I'll give you $500 a month for the next thirty years. Here's a check for $3,000 for your down payment. Anything else?"

"Heck, I don't know; don't you think we should sign something? I don't really have a pink slip or anything to prove that I'm giving you the title. And when will you get insurance?"

"Gee, I hadn't thought of that. . . . Well, those details will work themselves out eventually. Unless you can think of someone to call."

"No, I guess not. When did you want to move in?"

Ridiculous, you say? Not at all. We, the people, have found that the risks and rights of ownership must be clearly defined. The sole purpose of law is to allow society to impose order on itself. The complexity of the business of real estate is unfortunate, but the alternative is to invite chaos.

It became obvious hundreds of years ago that it would be impossible—or at least highly impractical—for every person who wanted to own real estate to know everything necessary for carrying out the transaction within the guidelines demanded by the law. It was only natural that specialists began to spring up to fill in the knowledge gap. Real estate agents specialize in getting buyers and sellers together; title officers specialize in searching title records and insuring the validity of title; real estate attorneys study for years so that they can guide people through the muddy and sometimes turbulent river of laws.

Real Estate Agents

I've already mentioned Realtors. As a broker, I understand the value of working with good real estate agents.

Why do we need agents? Because most of us cannot afford the time needed to learn even the fundamentals of buying and selling property. An agent, on the other hand, has developed an expertise; he or she has learned the basics and is part of an organization whose only reason for existence is to bring buyers and sellers together and make them feel comfortable buying and selling their homes. This is *not* information that we must depend on the agents for; every investor can learn just as much about buying and selling real estate as an agent. Again, it is only a matter of being willing to spend the time learning.

The agent offers something besides knowledge: As a part of a network of agents, the individual agent has access to listings of hundreds of anxious (and not-so-anxious) sellers in the area. In most counties there is a service, called the multiple listing service, that compiles a list of sellers who have contacted agencies asking for assistance in selling their homes. These services usually publish an MLS book, which the agents can use to locate properties for sale.

The agent, in putting sellers and buyers together, is providing a valuable service to the community. Without agents, few people would be willing to sell their homes to total strangers. Recognizing their value, agents charge their clients a commission (6 percent is common today in most parts of the country) for their service. On a $60,000 sale a 6 percent commission comes to $3,600, and agents expect to be paid in cash. They are working for the sellers, helping them sell their homes, and that means the sellers, not the buyers, must pay the commissions. But most sellers simply pass the extra charge to the buyers in the form of higher down payments.

As an investor, you should quickly reach a level where your expertise rivals—or surpasses—that of the best agents. And you will develop methods of locating anxious sellers, eliminating both advantages that agents have to offer. At that point you may never need the help of a real estate agent again, and commissions can be avoided.

Nevertheless, even when you have reached that level of knowledge, don't assume an agent has nothing to offer. I obtained 25 percent of all my purchases from referrals by real estate agents. They can help! Many of them know when a seller is anxious—when a seller has become a "don't wanter"—and not all of them (not even a majority of them) will be able or willing to take advantage of those situations themselves.

Even though an agent can be a great source of possible bargains, it is important that you understand the obligation an agent has toward the *seller*. He or she has a "fiduciary" responsibility; that is, a responsibility to act in the best interest of his or her client. So the agent is legally obligated to help the seller, and nobody is obliged to help the buyer.

I believe the newest phenomenon in the real estate marketplace is the **buyer's broker.** In most transactions there are two agents involved: the agent who listed the property for sale and the agent who actually found a buyer and sold the property. The two agents split the commission, which is paid by the seller. Therefore, both the listing and the selling agent are working for the seller, and both have a fiduciary responsibility to him or her. Because most sellers pass the expense of the commission to the buyer, both agents are working for the seller and are paid by the buyer.

There is a way that you, as the buyer, can turn the tables. Hire a broker yourself who will agree to find a property for you to buy. When the broker locates a house that is suitable for your needs, he or she will act as the selling agent but will be paid by you and will be acting in *your* best interests, not the seller's.

The commission is exactly the same as in the normal case because each agent will be paid half of the full commission. You will be paying your agent directly and the seller will be paying the listing agents. (Of course, that commission will probably be passed on to you anyway.)

By using a buyer's broker, you will have someone acting on your behalf, at no extra cost.

If you want to work with an agent, you'll have to do two

things: Find a good agent, and convince that agent that he or she should work with you.

Finding a good agent is usually a matter of finding an experienced, qualified expert. Like doctors or lawyers or any other professional, there is a wide variation in quality. All agents will be qualified to an extent. They have taken courses and have shown themselves to be qualified to represent buyers. How much training they must undergo varies widely from state to state, but in most states the fact that they have passed the necessary tests shows that they have enough knowledge to do a good job.

An agent who is a licensed member of a local real estate board affiliated with the National Association of Realtors is called a Realtor. Since an agent must undergo further training to qualify as a Realtor, you will often find that Realtors are more professional and knowledgeable than non-Realtor agents.

The perfect agent is a full-time professional, with a few years' experience and a high degree of self-motivation. He or she should understand creative finance and be willing to present creative offers.

How can you find the one-in-a-hundred agent who is all of the above and who will want to work with you? Well, how do you find a good doctor, or a good mechanic? Word of mouth still works best. Talk to the people who are most likely to know: other investors, mortgage lenders, friends who have recently bought or sold a home in the area, and real estate attorneys. Other investors are the first ones to ask. If they have managed to find a good agent and are willing to share, it will save you hours of searching. You can also call or visit realty offices in your area and talk to the agents yourself, but there is no real way to tell how good they are until you see them at work.

A good agent will give you access to the Multiple Listing Service and to hundreds of possible good deals. One investor I know has even formed a partnership with a Realtor. Whenever the Realtor spots what he thinks is a possibility, he calls the investor who immediately checks it out. Working together, they have bought and sold over one million dollars worth of real estate in the last two years.

Getting an agent to work with you may be a bigger challenge than finding the agent. To do so, you have to understand what makes agents tick. They are motivated by the same thing that pulls all of us out of bed in the morning and pushes us out the door: money. The commission earned by an agent—plus any job satisfaction experienced in bringing buyers and sellers together—is what prompts him or her to work hard making the sale. Here is where investors have difficulty in working with agents. As an investor you will have a narrow range of properties that will satisfy your needs. You are looking for houses that you can buy under market value, with little or nothing down, where you can assume the existing loan. No agent is going to want to spend hours trying to find those rarities—unless he or she is motivated.

Motivating an agent is a matter of proving that your relationship will be mutually profitable. After all, why would an agent call you with the perfect property when he or she can buy it? What can you offer that the agent needs or wants? Here are some advantages that you can provide:

You can find new listings. You will, of course, be calling and visiting houses that are for sale by owners. If they don't fit your needs, you can at least try to talk the sellers into listing their houses with an agent. Or you can call your agent and tell him or her where the house is located so he or she can try to get the listing.

You can agree to always use that agent. Even when you find a house for sale by owner and negotiate a contract yourself, you can still use your agent to assist you in finding a lender and closing the deal. A promise to always call your agent for his or her services is a good incentive for him or her to help you. And if you find a house listed by another agent, your agent can act as the selling broker—if the profit potential justifies the extra expense of the commission.

Your agent cannot buy all the good deals in town. If you present yourself as an anxious buyer, always willing to look into a possible deal, your agent will call you first every time a perfect deal comes along that he or she can't afford to buy. You may not have the money either, but as an investor you should be able to find someone, another investor or a partner, who does.

The first member of your team is an agent you can trust.

Real Estate Attorneys

A real estate attorney may be the most costly member of your investing team, and therefore the one you might think you can do without. After all, real estate contracts are pretty standard, and a Realtor can help you fill in the blank lines. Even the closing doesn't require an attorney; it can be taken care of in a title company office. So why incur the extra expense of an attorney?

If you want my opinion as to whether or not you must have a good real estate attorney on your team, you may be asking the wrong guy. Being a real estate attorney myself, I am rather biased toward my profession. So my first response is "Of course you do; if you didn't, I'd be out of work."

But there is more than self-preservation in my answer. Again and again I have stressed the same point: Experts are *experts*. They have spent years in highly specialized fields of study, and their expertise is what you lose if you fail to use them.

"Can I help you?"

"Yeah, I need to buy a set of tires for my car."

"What did you have in mind?"

"Gee, I don't know . . . what do you recommend?"

Everywhere you go you depend on expert advice. You ask the waiter which entree is best; you want the department store salesperson to tell you which refrigerator to buy. And when it comes time to make a $70,000 purchase, you had better avail yourself of the best real estate experts you can find.

I suppose that in reality you don't *have* to have a real estate attorney help you with your transaction any more than you *have* to have a doctor deliver your babies or a dentist fill your teeth. But buying real estate is so . . . *legal*. I seriously recommend that you surround yourself with experts who will stand by their expertise. A title officer can search the title and perform a closing, but his or her expertise stops short of being a legal expert. If there is a problem with the contract that surfaces later, who do you suppose will be responsible? The money spent in attorney's fees will be just one more part of a wise investment.

Finding an attorney isn't tough. Open the Yellow Pages and look in the "Attorneys" section. Then look in the subsection titled "Real Estate." Easy enough? Call the real estate attorneys and ask each one if they offer a free first-time consultation. If they do, sit down with them for a few minutes and describe your situation. Tell them honestly that you are a real estate investor looking for good deals. You're looking for a good attorney to help; someone you can trust, and someone you can call on whenever you have a legal question. Ask them to give you a call if they hear of a good deal—perhaps an upcoming foreclosure. In exchange for their help, you can promise to use their legal services exclusively in your real estate transactions.

Of course, not all attorneys were created equal. Finding the best attorney around may be difficult. Talk to other investors first; they will be happy to share their good and bad experiences with you. When you talk to the real estate attorneys in your area, don't be afraid to ask them for their qualifications. When did they graduate from law school, and where did they attend? When did they pass the bar? How long have they been practicing real estate law? I wouldn't mind answering any of those questions, and if an attorney seems to be avoiding your questions, feel free to look further.

For a free booklet on this subject titled *How to Choose and Use a Lawyer,* write the Consumer Information Center, Department 612M, Pueblo, Colorado 81009. This publication is filled with good ideas for finding a qualified attorney.

Other Investors

Many new investors fear competition from other, more experienced investors. What they don't realize is that their fears are completely groundless. Those other investors will be one of the best resources you have available for successful investing. The imagined disadvantage of having several investors in an area— that is, that competition will destroy your chances for success— is ridiculous. Every day thousands of home owners decide that it's time to sell. Out of those, at least 10 percent are "good deals." And no investor has enough money to buy every one that comes along.

Let me offer a few suggestions to you that will make life a lot easier as you get started.

1. *Join a local investors group.* You can do this by contacting an investors group in your area. They aren't that hard to find; attend the next real estate seminar that comes to town and you'll come into contact with enough fellow investors to keep you busy for a year. If you want to find out about the investment group closest to you, write to Jodestar Seminars, P.O. Box 562047, Miami, Florida 33256.

2. *Form partnerships with experienced investors.* Once you have met experienced investors, talk to one that you think you can work well with. Offer to call on ads, or visit home owners, or help in any other way. On the first couple of deals you work together, why not work for free? The first-hand education will be well worth a few hours work, and the more experienced investor will appreciate your help. After you start to catch on, suggest a partnership situation where you and your partner will split responsibilities, costs, and the profit.

3. *Form friendships with other investors.* One problem that you are going to encounter when you announce your intentions of becoming a real estate investor is that of well-intentioned friends who will do everything they can to stop you. "Oh, no," they might say, "someone told you that you could get rich quick in real estate. Well, Bob and Janice Looper lost their shirts in real estate, and you know what happened to Uncle Ted in 1977, and. . . ." It *is* hard to believe that you can succeed, and all it takes is a few words of discouragement to kill your dreams before they ever have a chance to live.

On the other hand, a few words of encouragement from someone who once wore your shoes and who now wears Gucci loafers can work wonders. I've found that not only are we judged by others by the company we keep, but we tend to judge ourselves by that company also. There is tremendous peer pressure on us that pulls us back down into the crowd whenever we threaten to take flight. If you want to soar with the eagles, you had better join their flock first and learn how to fly.

Title Officers

A title company exists for the sole purpose of tracing the chain of ownership of real property. For a fee you can have the title searched on any real estate you're buying; in fact, it is a requirement. Later in the book we'll look more closely at the concept of ownership and chains of title. For now, however, we'll concentrate on the next member of your investing team: a title officer.

A title officer is, obviously, someone who searches titles. In addition, title officers may conduct closings (check with a title officer in your state). If you do not have a real estate attorney, and if the title officer can conduct the closing, he or she may become an indispensable member of your team. Your title officer can actually help you with every piece of paperwork, from your first written offer to the last signature in triplicate. Even though title officers cannot give legal advice, they can certainly help you. If you develop a good working relationship with a title officer (by bringing some of your closings to his or her office), you can often get quick—and free—information for the cost of a phone call.

Call the title companies in your area (they are listed in the Yellow Pages) and ask them what they charge for a title search and for title insurance. Tell them you are considering an investment and you want to know their rates. Don't be afraid to ask any questions you have. How long does a title search take? What information do they need to begin searching the title? How much is title insurance, and what does it do for me, the buyer? This is a great opportunity to be taught by experts in your own town—for free!

Other Experts

While the experts mentioned above are all important, they aren't the only ones you'll need in the course of your investing career. Occasionally you will want to have a property professionally appraised—at least until you can appraise them yourself. You will also need to have properties inspected for everything from termites to structural damage, so an inspector will be added to your team. (We'll discuss inspectors and appraisers in more detail in the next chapter.)

All of these experts and more will be included on your roster of professionals. Work with them and learn from them. In many cases they will be happy to help you get started, knowing that you'll bring them future business and profits.

Don't think for a moment that you can—or should—act alone. You need a team behind you to take care of the details, leaving you free to find the good deals.

Makes sense, doesn't it?

Chapter Four Summary

1. Successful investing combines education, experience, newspapers, magazines, and team work. The education comes from books, seminars, workshops, and investor group meetings. Experience can only be gained in the field—talking to sellers, making offers, getting your hands dirty. Team work requires a *team* of professionals, and it's your responsibility to recruit your own team.

2. *Realtors* can, through their wide exposure to the market, put you in touch with sellers all across town. They can provide a high level of expertise in finding and dealing with motivated sellers. One good real estate agent can save you hours and hours of legwork.

3. *Real estate attorneys* can help in two ways: They can locate possible good deals, when they hear of

owners in trouble; and they can help you with any legal aspect of a transaction, from filling out a purchase offer to conducting the closing. Their advice won't come cheaply, but it will be well worth the expense.

4. *Other investors* aren't your competition; they're your teammates. They can't possibly buy every good deal in town, so why not work with them? An investors group is a great way to get—and stay—motivated, and you may even find another investor with whom you can form a partnership. Another investor may, in fact, be the most valuable player on your investing team.

5. *Title officers* are often overlooked by investors, and yet they can help you at every stage of the game. If you establish a good working relationship with at least one title officer, you'll be able to get free information with only a phone call.

6. *Other experts,* from appraisers to inspectors, are also only a phone call away. While not all of them will help you for free, their fees are reasonable, and if you look at the expense as tuition, it may be the least expensive education you'll ever have to pay for.

Chapter Four Homework

1. If your daily planner doesn't include a phone directory, buy one. Include in your directory at least one of each expert mentioned in this chapter.

2. Call real estate attorneys, agents, title officers, and other experts in your area. Introduce yourself as an investor and tell them you will be needing their help. Ask them what they can do for you in exchange for your exclusive use of their services.

3. Join an investors group. For the location of a group in your area, write to this address for recommendations:

Jodestar Seminars, Inc.
P.O. Box 562047
Miami, Florida 33256

Chapter Five

How To Investigate Property

It was another sultry, stormy night; raindrops the size of silver dollars threw themselves at my office window while lightning flashed angrily, lighting up the stack of unfinished work again and again. I was dog tired after a long day of detective work, but I'd had worse. Much worse. Being a P.I. is never an easy job, but a man does what a man has to do, and complaining never made the work any easier. I was reaching for the light switch, glad to call it a night, when she burst in without so much as a knock.

"Mr. Hunter," she panted, obviously out of breath, "you've got to help me!"

"What seems to be the problem, ma'am?" I took a good look; it'd been a while since I'd seen a dame with legs like that, and I wasn't about to kick her back into the storm that had already soaked her to the skin. I motioned to a chair and she took the hint, curling into it like it was made for her. She was still out of breath.

"It's my father, Mr. Hunter; I think the mob has kidnapped him to steal his secret formula, and I—" She broke off, sobbing.

"I'm sorry," I said reluctantly, "but there's not much I can do for you." It wasn't the first time someone had made the mistake.

"But your sign. It says Joe Hunter, P.I. If a private investigator can't help me, who can?"

"Sorry ma'am, but the P.I. stands for *property investigator.*"

It's a dirty job, but somebody's got to do it.

You'll be spending this chapter learning how to investigate real estate, how to uncover the hidden defects that may lie in wait. This chapter and the next (on working with the sellers) have something important in common: They both deal with digging deeper and deeper into a possible transaction. You should, at this point, be able to sift through the many properties for sale each week and spot the few promising deals. You should also have a team of experts "on call," waiting to help you. Now it's time to put on your deerstalker, pick up the magnifying glass, and take a close look.

Before we get into the heart of property investigation, let's take a break (if you've been applying yourself, you've earned it). The following quiz is applicable to the subject at hand: Each question, like a promising property, may be misleading.

(Answers at the end of the chapter.)

The Obvious Quiz

1. What is catgut?
2. Where are Panama hats made?
3. What does the distress signal SOS stand for?
4. In what country did dachshunds originate?
5. How long was the Hundred Years' War?
6. How much does a ten-gallon hat hold?
7. What color is the purple finch?
8. How many zeroes are there in a billion?

9. How many "witches" were burned in Salem, Massachusetts?

10. What animals were the Canary Islands named after?

11. What was King George VI's first name?

12. How long was the Thirty Years' War?

As the quiz illustrates, there may often be more than meets the eye—something to keep in mind as you delve further into what at first looks like a good deal. I firmly believe that you shouldn't allow minor details and groundless fears to stop you from pursuing a good deal, but for your own sake, don't take everything at face value. In this chapter and the next, you'll learn where to look, how to look, and what questions to ask.

Investigating the Property

Finding out all the information you'll need to know about a particular piece of property can be a tough job. We'll go through the process step-by-step, from the minute you locate a potential good deal to the last day of escrow.

Take a Good Look

First item of business: inspecting the property.

Your inspection of the house will usually be in three phases: a cursory inspection that will probably take less than a half hour; a more thorough inspection, getting down on your hands and knees now and then; and a professional inspection for hidden defects.

The first time you approach a new house, begin your inspection before you even pull up to the curb. "Curb appeal" is a term used to describe the general attractiveness that a house has as you approach it. A lack of curb appeal can greatly diminish the value of a home because home owners are looking for a place where they can be proud to hang their hats. I recently looked at a house that was absolutely gorgeous inside. The walls were newly papered in beautifully coordinated patterns; the layout was perfect for the size of the house; the previous owners had evidently poured many hour and dollars into making the most of their home. But driving up to the house was, to say the least, disconcerting. The next-door neighbor's motorcycle was parked on the lawn because the hot rod on blocks took up most of the driveway and the open garage was too cluttered to allow any parking space. Across the street, next to the printing shop and the auto shop, was a large apartment complex that looked semi-abandoned and forbidding. The house I was looking at was well tended, but it was quite old, and the general air of the neighborhood gave me an uneasy feeling. I didn't have any intention of living in it anyway, but I knew that it would be almost impossible to sell to anyone more civilized than a band of Hell's Angels.

Visit the house during the middle of the day, if possible, to catch it in full daylight. When you meet the owners they will be expecting you to walk through, so feel free to ask them for a tour. It isn't necessary—and it would be a waste of time for both you and the owners—to go over each room with a fine-tooth comb at this point. Instead, look at the general layout and try to get a feel for the house. Is there enough cupboard space in the kitchen? Is the lighting adequate? How old is the house? What problems have the sellers had with it? Your questions should invite comment from the sellers, and the whole time you are walking and talking you should be trying to look through the eyes of the person who will be living there soon—your buyer or your tenant. Don't be distracted by things that can be easily remedied, such as dirty carpets and marks on the walls. And don't be so overwhelmed by the the beautiful wallpaper that you ignore the lousy layout; one can be changed in a day, the other will be there forever.

Walk outside and look at the yard. How much work is needed? (A lawn mower in the hands of a capable neighborhood kid can bring the selling price up a thousand dollars.) Is there a sprinkler system, or will the next owners be dragging a hose around the yard all summer? Does the house need to be repainted?

By the time you have walked through and around the house, talking about features, price, and terms, you will at least have formed the basis for a decision as to whether or not you want to pursue the deal. If you have been doing your homework, and have at least an idea of market values, you will be ready to begin serious negotiating. If you've decided to pass up this house, it's on to the next without too much time spent.

If you are impressed enough by your cursory inspection, stop by again that night and take a look at the house and the neighborhood. Some areas look great during the day, only to change into something sinister at night. Are the streets well lit? Are there loud parties next door? Is there any reason at all that a buyer would be hesitant to live there, day or night? If so, be careful. You won't make any money investing in real estate if you can't find a buyer or a renter.

If you've decided, after the first visit, to seriously look at the house, call the owners and set a time when you can make a more thorough inspection. Before arriving, you should determine your negotiating range: what price and terms you want, and what you would be willing to settle for. Take a purchase offer with you and be prepared to make a bona fide offer after the inspection.

Have the owner accompany you as you look at the house, so you can ask questions. Every fault you find will probably mean a lower price.

Appliances: Ask which appliances are to be included in the sale, and make sure they are specified in the contract. If the owner still has any warranties or service agreements, be sure to get the paperwork before the closing.

Heating and Air Conditioning: If you are inspecting in the dead of winter, you will no doubt find out how good the heating system is, but you might not check the air conditioning. Turn off the heater and start the conditioner running; in summer, do the opposite. Look at the heater itself and inspect the pipes. If they look old, chances are they *are* old and may need to be replaced soon.

The Attic: If the house has an attic, this is the place to inspect the insulation. If it is less than three inches thick, you will probably want to add more. Mention this fact to the seller; the additional cost to you should be deducted from the selling price.

The Basement: The pressure from the rest of the house will show up down here. Stand at a doorway and sight along the wall. Check the ceiling and the floor for straightness; any sagging or warping could be a sign of structural weakness. Is the floor level, or is it noticeably lower in places? A sinking basement floor can mean real trouble.

The Ceilings and Walls: Look for water spots on every ceiling, upstairs and down. Brownish, discolored circles are usually indications of water leakage and roof problems. Also look for sagging in the ceiling. When you look at the walls, look for cracks, inside and out. Small hairline fractures are normal, but if you can put your little finger into the crack you may be looking at serious structural damage.

Plumbing: Turn on every faucet, inside and out, to check the water pressure. Flush every toilet. Open every cupboard under every sink and look for water of signs of leakage. Try both the hot and cold water on every tap. In one house I inspected, every faucet seemed to work great, until I tried the hot water in the kitchen sink. There was a leak—maybe a drop every second— in the hot water pipe, so the seller had turned off the hot water under the sink before showing it to me. A drop every second can add tremendously to your monthly heating bill, and catching it in a bucket under the sink isn't the answer. Plumbing can be a major expense, even for seemingly minor leaks.

Lighting: Turn on every light in every room, especially the kitchen. If the kitchen still resembles a cavern at midnight, you will need to install new lights before you try to sell or rent the house. The kitchen, more than any other room, will be the key to the house's "sellability." Also check the outside lighting: Is it sufficient for safety's sake? Is the back yard lit well enough for a lazy summer night's barbecue?

Doors: Open and close every door, even the closet doors. Do they open easily, or do they need two strong men to pry them open? When they are partway open do they swing open or shut, or do they stay where they are put? This problem may be easily remedied, but a few well placed "um hummms" as you kick the door gently shut will give you a bargaining chip.

Windows: Do they all open and close easily? How well do they fit? In most parts of the country, where cold weather prevails all winter, a poorly fitted window can cost dearly. And a window that won't open at all can be a nuisance, as well as a danger in case of fire.

General Age and State of Repair: If the owner isn't sure how old the house is, you can usually get an idea by checking the inside of the toilet tanks. The company that made the toilet will stamp the date of manufacture either on the inside of the lid or the inside of the tank. Since most toilets are built in when the house is constructed, you can get an accurate estimate of its age.

Defects

Every flaw that you can find in a property is a bargaining tool which, when wielded properly, can be many dollars off the purchase price.

Point out deficiencies, such as discolored spots on the ceiling, to the owner and ask about them. "Gee, it looks like you've had a little trouble with rain here." Or, "Of course, I'll have to slap a coat of paint on these walls before I can use the house; how much were you going to take off for that?" Be just as friendly and polite as possible, but let the sellers know that you expect a discount to make up for the trouble you are going to have to go through to correct the problems.

A few common problems to look for and comment on:

landscaping (or lack of)

bugs and ticks in the carpet from pets

run-down appliances

threadbare carpeting

chipped, peeling, and faded paint

any other signs of poor maintenance

Make it obvious that you had anticipated that the asking price was for a house in good condition, and that anything that might diminish your expectations must be corrected by them or dealt with in the form of a price reduction. Do not pass up the opportunity to put this powerful tool to work for you.

Look at *everything* in every room, and inspect the house thoroughly around the outside. Don't stop asking questions; it may be the only time you really look things over before making an offer, and price concessions usually follow an inspection that uncovers faults. Don't be overbearing, or you will lose the goodwill of the seller. But don't be afraid to politely point out problems and ask for explanations.

Another suggestion, after you have made your inspection but before making the offer: Ask the seller for records that pertain to maintenance costs. If the winter gas bills or summer electricity bills are very high, the insulation may be inadequate. Here is a short list of questions that you should always ask:

How much is your monthly electric bill? Does it vary from one season to the next?

Do you have copies of your bills?

How much is your gas bill each month, and how much does it vary?

Was there a rate increase in your utilities last year; how much?

Are you on a public sewer or a septic tank?

If you are on a septic tank, when was it last cleaned out?

Who maintains your yard? (You may get an excellent recommendation here for a neighborhood kid who is happy to do a good job for extra money.)

Gas, electricity, water, yard work, and any other maintenance or utility services will become your concern when the property is yours. The sellers will already be familiar with those costs and will have receipts from previous bills that they can show you. If they are unwilling to cooperate, a red flag should be waving and I urge caution.

Once you have made this inspection, you should be ready to sit down and negotiate with the seller. You will be armed with enough knowledge about the property to make a reasonable offer, and the seller knows it. However, you will want to reserve the right to have a professional inspection before closing. That way, if any hidden defects later surface, the seller will be held responsible for them. To give yourself that right, include the following clauses in your offer:

Prior to closing, the Buyer shall, at his expense, have a right to have a roof, seawall [where applicable], pool, electrical, mechanical, and plumbing inspection made by persons or campanies qualified and licensed to perform such services. If such inspection reveals defects, Seller shall pay all costs of repairing said defects, and if repairs are not complete prior to closing, sufficient funds shall be escrowed at time of closing to effect said repairs.

Prior to closing, at Buyer's expense, the Buyer shall have the right to have the property inspected by a licensed exterminating company to determine whether there is any active termite or wood-destroying organism present in any improvements on said property, or any damage from prior termite or wood-destroying organism to said improve-

ments. If there is any such infestation or damage, the Seller shall pay all costs of treatment and repairing and/or replacing all portions of said improvements which are infested or have been damaged.

In the next chapter we'll talk in more detail about negotiating, and you'll see even more clearly how vital this second inspection is to consummating a good deal.

The most important part of your inspection will be *asking* the seller every question that comes to mind. As you are touring the house in the company of the owner, *always* ask, "Is there anything wrong with this house that I should know about that you haven't told me?" You may have to prepare yourself for a shock: Most sellers are honest, and they will go out of their way to admit their property's faults—if you ask.

Usually when the question is put to the owners, they will stop and think for a moment, trying to come up with an answer. The question seems to call for more than a simple "No, the house is perfect," and they will often come up with something, no matter how trivial, to answer your query.

The $500 Question

I asked the question of an owner while inspecting a house just prior to closing. I was satisfied that everything was in order; we agreed on everything, I had had the property professionally inspected, and I was eager to sign the papers. On a hunch (and out of practice) I asked, "Is there anything else that might be wrong with the house that you haven't told me about yet?" I asked it in a tone that, while friendly, suggested that there might indeed be a fault and it was his last chance to confess.

His response was surprising. He pointed out one of the eaves overlapping the doorway that had always leaked. I had paid for a roof inspection but the roofer never caught the problem. Now, one hour before closing, the seller was suddenly willing to tell me all about it. I immediately called the roofer and demanded that he reinspect that property and call me at the closing. Lo and behold, the phone call came during the closing and the roofer informed me that there was a problem, and it would cost an additional $500 for repairs. He rushed over to the closing with an inspection report. The seller gave me a $500 credit to cover the cost and the problem was solved—because I had asked one simple question.

The question by itself is no substitute for a professional inspection, but the minor problems that have been bothering the sellers for years will often come to light under a little friendly interrogation.

Recently the board of Realtors in my area initiated the following clause to be inserted into their contracts:

> *The seller represents that he knows of no facts ma-terially affecting the value or desirability of the property which are not readily observable, except the following:* _____
> _____.

A similar type of clause in your purchase contract which would, of course, be signed by the seller, would certainly be recommended.

Professional Inspections

After the acceptance of your offer, but before the closing (during the **escrow period**), you should have the property professionally inspected. This inspection will reveal defects that might not be apparent to your untrained eye, and the uncovering of a hidden defect before closing could save you thousands.

Finding an inspector is simple. Open the Yellow Pages to either "Property Inspection" or "Inspection Services." If you can't find a listing in either place, call a title officer or real estate agent and ask for assistance. The fees for inspections vary, and in some cases may seem high, but like most costs associated with real estate investing, the expense is well justified.

It's a good idea to walk around the house with the inspector, asking questions as you go. You will learn what to look for, and it will make your future house-hunting much more profitable. After the inspection, review any problems with the inspector. Ask him or her for advice—everyone likes to be respected for their expertise—and for a rough idea of the repair costs involved.

The inspector is another professional to add to your team. He can tell you a property's problems and can even suggest the best ways to solve those problems. Once you've located a problem you can begin estimating how much its solution will cost. Call a repairman and ask for a written estimate. I like to have the seller give me a credit toward the cost of repairs, rather than insist that he or she complete them. That gives me better control over the quality of the repair work, and I can often get the work done for less than the estimate, effectively lowering the price of the property. In fact, I have the credit applied toward the down payment, which saves cash at closing.

Some sellers will recognize the fact that they can save—or make—the same money, and they may want to do the repairs themselves. If the seller insists on paying for the repairs, don't go to closing until they have been completed and reinspected.

You should have your phone book out by now, finding a property inspector. Find out *right now* how you can set up an appointment for an inspection and how much it will cost. Then, when you actually need an inspection, you'll be ready.

You will, before you're through, actually subject the property to four inspections: your first drive-by, curbside inspection, as you form your first impression; a quick walk-through inspection, looking for layout, amenities, and easily noticed features; a more thorough, careful room-by-room inspection with the seller as your guide, asking in-depth questions; and a professional inspection to reveal hidden (and costly) defects.

That's a lot of inspecting, but you still won't know everything you need to know about the property. You must also carefully appraise its true market value and plan for its future.

The Appraisal

The most basic appraisal is the one you've already learned: general market value. You should have learned your market well enough to know whether a house in question is under- or overpriced—at least if it's off by more than a few thousand dollars.

If a house looks as though it will sell below market value, you can ask the sellers how they arrived at their asking price. They may be your best bet for finding out the house's market value. It's not uncommon for them to say something like "It was appraised by the bank six months ago at $75,000, and we're willing to sell it for only $70,0000 to get rid of it." A bank appraisal is usually a dependable indicator of value. On the other hand, many sellers go by a real estate agent's curbside appraisal, which may or may not be accurate. And, least accurate of all is the response, "Well, the house across the street sold for $76,000 and ours has an extra bathroom, so we figured it must be worth at least $80,000."

If you have a friendly Realtor you can call on, he or she may be willing to render an opinion, especially if you are working together as an investment team. A Realtor's appraisal is only a second opinion, but as a preliminary estimate it will help you weed out unprofitable deals.

If everything looks good at this stage, the next step is a more careful appraisal, based on comparable properties. This will require a higher degree of sophistication on your part, and a lot more work than your first impression, but here is where the real appraising begins.

Comparable Appraisal

1. Find three properties similar to the subject property that have been sold recently (within six months). They should have the same basic features, such as number of bedrooms and bathrooms, and the size of the lots should be about equal. They must also be located in similar neighborhoods. Your

Realtor friend can help you here by supplying three such properties, or you can find them yourself by watching the market closely.

2. Set up a table listing all three comparables and the subject property. Compare them feature by feature, adjusting the value of the comparables to match the subject property. For example, if one of the comparables has a built-in sprinkler system, and your subject property does not, you should subtract the cost of such a system from the selling price of the comparable property.

	Comparable
Selling price:	$68,500
Sprinklers	− 500
Adjusted Value	$68,000

3. After adjusting the sales prices of the three comparables, add their adjusted prices together and divide by three (take their average). The resulting average price will be a very accurate market value for your subject property.

As I warned, it isn't an easy process. But it is a process used by every professional appraiser.

If you're not ready or able to appraise accurately your own properties, you should by all means hire a professional appraiser. He will charge a hundred to two hundred dollars for his opinion, but that opinion is based on extensive experience and will be a reliable estimate. If, after your own curbside appraisal and personal inspection, it looks like you're onto a good thing, then I would certainly advise you to put up a hundred dollars or more to investigate further.

Estimating Fix-Up Costs

Properties that need a little work—"fixers"—are, as I've already mentioned, excellent investments. But how much will it cost you to do the fixing? A mistake in estimating fix-up expenses may cost you all of your projected profits.

Which repairs qualify as low-cost, high-return fix-ups? I recommend looking for the following:

Wallpaper works wonders. A bright, sunny design in the kitchen will brighten the whole house; in bedrooms, a pattern that makes the most of the carpet color. Beware of dark colors; they tend to make a room look smaller and more gloomy.

Trim paint will make the exterior look like new. I've seen old, washed-out houses suddenly restored to life by just a touch of trim paint, and if you are at all handy with a brush, one Saturday will be enough to make a house sparkle.

Flower pots from a nursery are relatively inexpensive, and they only take a minute to put in place. Fresh flowers will make the whole yard look healthy.

Brighter lights in the house will help it sell, especially in the kitchen. Don't use a powerful bulb in a lamp that wasn't made to withstand the heat, but make sure that every socket has a working light in it, and replace low-wattage bulbs with brighter ones.

Lawn care is generally a low-cost item that should be near the top of your list. A dying lawn can be brought back to life quickly with water and fertilizer, and an overgrown lawn only needs a mower (I recommend renting a large enough mower to really tackle the job). Watch out for completely dead yards; replanting is time- and money-consuming.

Dirty carpets look horrible but usually cost very little to clean. Call a carpet cleaner and ask for a bid. Buyers looking for a place to live will be disgusted with dirty carpets, and sellers in trouble are often unwilling to bear the expense. By spending a hundred dollars or less on carpet cleaning, you may increase the sales price of the home by several hundred, even a thousand. Watch out for carpets that need to be replaced; they may not pay equal returns.

Get creative! As you inspect the house begin taking mental notes; in every room try to think of at least one inexpensive improvement that might increase the selling price.

Fixing up properties might not be your idea of a glamorous way to make money—certainly not as exciting or as sophisticated as trading silver futures—but as a way to begin building a fortune it has been shown by countless real estate tycoons to be one of the very best.

Income Property

While this book isn't geared toward buying apartment complexes, you may want to buy houses or multi-unit complexes that have been used as rental properties. The following section will help you estimate possible rental cash flow.

If you are thinking about investing in a large multi-unit complex, two questions should be answered: Are you ready for the financial, mental, and emotional pressure that such a property can exert; and, second, if the property is already making good money, why would the owner want to sell?

If you have asked both questions—the first of yourself and the second of the seller—and have found satisfactory answers, continue. If not, consider your move carefully; this may not be as easy or lucrative as it appears.

The following is an unhappy experience that I read about in a local paper.

A Realtor-investor purchased a forty-unit apartment complex. He was probably excited about its track record: three years without a vacancy! Without vacancies the gross receipts amounted to $144,000 per year. He also received a profit-and-loss statement for the previous six-month period and copies of all the leases.

He closed the transaction in December, and when January 1 rolled around he stopped by each apartment. He introduced himself as the new owner, wished his tenants a Happy New Year, and asked for the rent. Every tenant refused to pay. After about twenty doors he finally got up the nerve to ask why they weren't paying the rent. He was understandably shocked to find out that the previous owner had never collected rent in January; his Christmas present to his valued tenants was one rent-free month every year.

The new owner was in a quandary. He could try to enforce the lease, which called for a monthly payment, and ignore the custom of a rentless month; he could evict every tenant, emptying his new building; he could follow custom and lose $12,000; or he could sue the previous owner for fraud. Guess which one he chose?

The old owner was forced to take back the property and pay damages for his misrepresentation, so the story does have at least a satisfactory ending, if not a happy one. But that investor learned one more lesson: Always ask—no, demand—a profit-and-loss statement for at least one full year previous, and insist on a copy of all rental records for as far back as possible.

Not all sellers are honest; nor are they all dishonest. Checking the veracity of their statements isn't a sign of distrust on your part; it's just good business sense. The seller will surely have kept good records; after all, owning a multi-unit property is a business. If records have not been kept, you might want to steer clear of that property.

The best way to ensure that you will enjoy the profit the seller claims you will is to ask for a **guaranteed rent role** (or "performance mortgage").

Have the seller give you a written guarantee that the gross rental income will be X amount, and that the expenses will not exceed Y. That guarantees Z, your net profit. If the actual profit is less than Z, the seller will give you a credit for the difference and deduct that from the money you owe on the property.

The guaranteed rent role will stop a dishonest seller in his tracks. If he has been making unwarranted claims, he will never be willing to back them up with his own money, will he? On the other hand, if the seller is honest neither of you will have anything to worry about.

Since we're talking about rental properties, let's go to the other people involved: the tenants. They can provide a wealth of information about the sellers. I always interview the tenants before I even begin any serious negotiating. Here are just a few questions that I ask:

Is the management responsive to your needs?

Is the management on the premises full time?

What is wrong with the property?

Is the building well maintained?

Is there enough heat in winter?

How well is the swimming pool maintained?

Are repairs made promptly?

Are there any problems with crime in the area?

Does the management allow loud noises from the neighbors in the middle of the night?

Do you feel safe?

You can no doubt come up with many more questions that apply in each case. The idea is to have the tenants help you look at the property through their eyes. The pluses and minuses they uncover will help tremendously when you are negotiating with the seller.

In addition to a guaranteed rent role, you should request permission to review all pertinent records including the owner's profit-and-loss statements for at least the previous five years. If you encounter reluctance, beware!

Another problem you may encounter when buying income property is the seller's failure to collect past-due rents. Include in your contract a clause that makes collection of rent prior to closing the sole responsibility of the seller. Also make sure that any rents collected during the final month of the sale are prorated so you get your fair share of the rental income for that month. Here is the clause that I always include in an offer to purchase rental property:

> *Rents, as shown on the rental statement furnished by Seller, and approved by Buyer, are to be prorated to (a specific date or the closing date for this agreement). Seller will collect all rents which fall due prior to the close of this agreement. There shall be no adjustment against the Buyer on uncollected rents.*

I once represented a man who was buying three four-plexes (12 units total). The rent on each unit was $400, for a total gross income of $4,800 a month. The seller's attorney and I worked out the details of the transaction and I told my client exactly how much he would need to bring to the closing, which he did. He arrived at the closing with a cashier's check for the correct amount, so it was a surprise to my client, the other attorney, and myself when the seller looked at the check and said, "There must be some mistake here. This should be $14,400 more." When we recovered sufficiently to ask him for an explanation, he informed us that he had not collected rents during the entire three-month escrow period, and he wanted that rental income. He was expecting the buyer to pay him $14,400 and then try to collect it from the tenants. Fortunately, we had included the clause I just gave you, and the seller was forced to collect the rents himself.

Finding Tenants

You'd hate to buy a multi-unit apartment with vacancies, wouldn't you? Or, for that matter, if you're buying a single-family house with the intention of renting it, it would be great to have a tenant lined up and ready to move in the day of closing, wouldn't it?

If you haven't yet purchased the property, there is a simple solution that is especially effective for an apartment complex: Include in your contract a clause stipulating that the current owner must find a suitable tenant before you close on the property. You must have the right to approve prospective tenants, and you must agree not to withhold your approval unreasonably. That will ensure that you have the type of tenant you are looking for.

I used this clause on a single-family house I was buying as a rental property. I never had to show the house myself, and the former owner got my first tenant for me. I closed the transaction on December 30, my tenant moved in December 31, and I never missed one day's rent.

With one simple clause you have transferred the problem back to the present owner and eliminated the worry. And you can tie up the property for the entire escrow period without binding yourself to it until you have a good tenant lined up.

The seller of a house may not be willing to find your tenant for you, but that shouldn't stop you from finding one yourself. You have any rights that you have given yourself in the purchase offer that the seller signs. Of course you will want to show the property; that's true whether you are going to show it to prospective tenants or buyers. A popular method of investing is to "flip" properties. When you flip a property, you tie it up with a purchase offer and then show it and sell it prior to closing, either by assigning the contract or by using a double closing.

The clause that will do the trick here is a simple one-liner that no seller should find objectionable: *Buyer has the right to show this property to prospective tenants or buyers from the date of acceptance of this offer until date of closing.*

This is a very important clause to include if you are going to have a long escrow period; it gives you the right to find the person who will be giving you your profit. And that makes perfect sense, doesn't it?

Chapter Five Summary

I. Finding what looks like a good deal isn't enough; before you can make an offer you must subject the property to inspections and appraisals to assure yourself you are buying right.

II. Property inspection includes:
   A. A cursory inspection when you're walking through for the first time. You don't need to get down on your hands and knees and check every corner during this inspection; all you want is a first impression.
   B. A second, much closer look, in which you will question the owner about every defect you can find. This is the beginning of your actual negotiations, and concessions won during this inspection tour can save thousands of dollars. This will be your last inspection before making a written offer, so take your time and look carefully.
   C. A professional inspection during the escrow period. Walking through with the inspector and asking questions is a great way to get a free education.

III. Appraising the property is a necessary part of getting a good deal. Don't take the seller's word for the property's value, and don't rely solely on your limited curbside appraisal. Get a second opinion from a professional appraiser, or at least conduct your own appraisal, based on the selling prices of comparable properties.

IV. Estimate fix-up costs before you make your offer. Learn to recognize low-cost repairs that will pay big dividends, and avoid major restorations that won't increase the selling price enough to offset their costs.

V. If you're buying income-producing property, get as much information from the previous owner as possible. Demand a guaranteed rent role and calculate rental income. Estimate management costs, tax savings, and vacancy factor; if you're still left with positive cash flow, buy it. Insist that the seller either find your tenants for you or give you the right to show the property. You must do all of the above in order to *buy right*.

Chapter Five Homework

1. It's time to do more than drive by. Closely inspect at least one potential deal this week. Make a list of repairs that need to be made and estimate their costs. Decide now how much you would offer for the property as is, and how much you think it will sell for when fixed up. Will the cost of repairs be a good investment? How much return would you expect from your investment?

2. Find out the names and telephone numbers of an inspector and an appraiser. Include them in your telephone directory.

3. Appraise at least one property on your own, using three recently-sold houses for comparison. This may be the hardest assignment so far, but it will be well worth the effort. If you have trouble locating three comparable properties, ask your Realtor for help. He or she should have access to a quarterly listing of houses that have been sold through the listing service.

Answers to Quiz:

1. Catgut is a tough cord made from the intestines of sheep and horses.

2. Panama hats are made in Ecuador.

3. SOS doesn't actually stand for anything. It is merely a code that is easy to tap out in Morse code.

4. The dachshund breed of dogs originated in ancient Egypt, not in Germany, as the name may lead one to believe.

5. The Hundred Years' War lasted 115 years—from 1338 to 1453.

6. A ten-gallon hat will hold about three quarts.

7. A purple finch's plumage is predominantly a brilliant red.

8. In the United States, Canada, and France, a billion is a thousand million: 1,000,000,000; in Great Britain and Germany, a billion is a million million: 1,000,000,000,000. So how many zeroes there are in a billion depends upon *where* you are when you define it.

9. Nobody was burned in the famous witch trials of Salem; nineteen women were hanged and one was stoned to death.

10. The Canary Islands were named after a breed of dogs indigenous to the area. The islands were named in Latin, *Insularia Canaria:* "Island of Dogs."

11. King George VI's first name was Albert. In taking the name George he was deferring to Queen Victoria's wish that no king of England be named Albert.

12. The Thirty Years' War took place from 1618 to 1648— thirty years, of course!

Chapter Six

The Sellers

Now we come to what beginning investors seem to fear the most: the dreaded *sellers*. So far we've only had to deal with solid, unemotional, inanimate buildings. You can't hurt a building's feelings, and it can't hurt yours. You can't harass a house or antagonize an apartment. But a seller; well, that's another story altogether.

When Mr. Home Owner says, "We really love our old home. Why, Grandmother Wilkinson died right there in that green chair by the fireplace," your reaction may not be, "Oh goody; now I'll offer twice as much as I would have!" So you've got a problem: perceived value versus real value. The solution is in looking at the negotiation from both sides of the table at once, and getting Mr. Home Owner to do the same.

There are several keys to successfully negotiating a price:

Find out the sellers' *needs*, not *wants*.

If there is one key for negotiating that you must learn, it's the necessity to find out *needs*, not *wants*.

Everybody *wants* cash. J. Paul Getty had a pay phone in his home for his guests to use, but he certainly didn't need the cash.

It's simple in concept, but actually putting it to use may prove to be difficult in some situations. Sellers often perceive their own wants as needs. Like a child who "needs" a cookie, the seller may be convinced that he needs his entire equity in cash.

Sometimes all you have to do is ask. When the seller has $15,000 equity in his property, and insists on receiving the full amount in cash, ask him what he intends to do with that much cash. The most common response is "I am going to be buying a new home and I need the money for a down payment and a few things we will be needing."

Analyze his stated use for the money. How much will he really need as a down payment on his new house? It's unlikely that he needs the full amount for the down payment, and many of those "things" could be bought with payments—payments that you would be making to him every month.

Occasionally you will find a seller whose answer is "What I do with the money is none of your business!" I've had more than one seller say that, and my response is "It's my money, and I think I have the right to know what happens to it. If I don't know what my money is going to be used for, then I'm not interested in purchasing your home." Such a response may sound too abrupt, but there are too many excellent bargains waiting to be bought to spend much time with unmotivated sellers.

Nobody has enough money to make large down payments forever; even a multi-millionaire will run out of money eventually if he has to put $10,000 down on every property he buys. The key to successful investing is to tie up as little of your money as possible and still have the price and the payments stay low enough to make each investment profitable. In many cases that means convincing the sellers that they should allow you to make monthly payments for their equity.

The trick to convincing the sellers to accept payments is to find out their *needs*. If their equity is, for example, $20,000, do they actually need $20,000 cash? Does *anybody* actually need that much cash all at once? Of course not! So how much do they really need, and what do they need the money for? If they won't answer those questions, then they really aren't yet members of that elite club we call "don't wanters." Membership is only by motivation (sometimes called desperation), and if they aren't motivated enough to give you the information you need then they aren't motivated enough to sell to you. Check back in another month if the property isn't sold by then.

If you find out that they *need* $5,000 for a down payment on a new home, you have a great place to start negotiating. Explain that if they will accept payments on the remaining equity, they will be earning interest on the money every month.

If the sellers remain unconvinced it may be time to look elsewhere. There is no need to spend fruitless hours talking to unmotivated sellers, and there is even less need to tie up large amounts of cash in every property.

Concentrate on minor issues.

If you are sitting down at the kitchen table with the sellers and you're talking price, you may suddenly find yourselves at an impasse. You're not about to go any higher, and they won't go lower. What can you do? The best tactic is to drop the area of contention for a while and concentrate on some of the less important issues. You could say, "Let's come back to the price later. I'd like to talk about the appliances that are going to be included." Often the simple step of finding other areas of agreement will break down barriers before they become real obstacles.

Trade concessions.

A second idea is to gain a concession for every one given. Don't get stuck on price when there are so many other aspects of the bargain. You could agree to pay the extra $3,000, but only if you could do so in 48 monthly installments, with no interest, starting in one year. Or only if all of the appliances would be included and the seller would pay all closing costs. Or. . . .
In other words, give in without actually giving anything away.

Use time pressure.

After you've spent several hours with a particular seller, talking about the house, inspecting it, and talking again, time begins to work for you. Look the seller in the eye, smile wistfully, shrug your shoulders, and say: "Gee, it's too bad that we're not going to get together on the price. We've spent so much time together, and I was really looking forward to reaching an agreement today. What a shame to have all that time wasted when we're only $3,000 apart. We've worked together for, gosh, about four hours, and I thought for sure we would be able to get together. Only $3,000. . . . Oh well, I suppose there will be another buyer, and I'm sure you'll be able to get your price. But what a shame, only $3,000. . . ." In other words, emphasize all the time and effort that both of you have expended and stress the price difference. Show that, although you wish you could agree, you are ready and willing to give up.

Nine times out of ten this last tactic will prompt the other person to offer to "split the difference." If you were stuck at an offer of $45,000 and the seller was insisting on $48,000, you may suddenly hear, "Well, let's just split the difference." That's your opportunity to make your best and last offer. You respond with: "Split the difference, hmm? That means you would be willing to accept $46,500 . . . and I am offering $45,000. That's great; now we're only $1,500 apart, and I'm sure we can reach an agreement." You haven't actually accepted the split at all, have you? And yet you have forced the seller to give up $1,500 of his or her negotiating range.

There is always room for negotiation; if not in price, then in some other area. Do not allow that all-important price tag to keep you from thinking creatively and finding creative solutions to apparent impasses.

Establish your negotiating range.

If you find that you're suddenly about to offer more for a property than you think it's worth, you can be sure you're making two mistakes: You're falling in love with the property, which you've already been warned against; and you failed to establish a **negotiating range.**

Establish your range and stick to it. Whether you are buying or selling, and whether the item negotiated for is a $50 necklace in a jewelry store or a $500,000 piece of property, decide *in advance* what your lowest and highest price will be and then be willing to walk away if you can't reach an agreement within that range.

If the house you were thinking about buying had a market value of $50,000, you may have decided that you'd be willing to pay as much as $48,000, so you offered $47,900. You started at the top of your negotiating range, instead of the bottom, and in doing so you gave yourself absolutely no room for concession.

Wrong, wrong, wrong. *Never* give your very best offer up front; you will be giving away your entire negotiating range and the deal will collapse. And if your opponent will not raise (or lower, if you are the buyer) his or her price to within your range, be prepared to walk away from the deal.

When you looked at that house worth $50,000, you should have decided that the most you would pay would be $48,000; you actually want to pay $46,000, and you'd love to get it for $44,000, although you never think the seller will accept such a low offer. By starting at $44,000 you're allowing yourself $4,000 negotiating room.

Good guy/Bad guy

Occasionally you may face a seller who inspects your offer and then says, "Well, it looks good, but I'll have to have my wife (husband, mother-in-law, best friend's next-door neighbor's second cousin) approve it before I can sign. If this ever happens (and it will), your seller will be using one of the oldest—and best—negotiating tactics: the invisible partner. The reason such a tactic is so effective is that there is little you can do to combat its use. When you make a written offer and the seller says, "I can't sign this without so-and-so's approval," what can you say? You are left with either accepting those terms or revoking your offer.

Nine times out of ten the approving party will play the bad guy, refusing your offer and forcing you to renegotiate. You are put on the defensive, and you are likely to give up a good portion of your negotiating range if you fall victim to this tactic.

The best way to counter this strategy is by foreseeing it. Before you present your written offer, call the seller and make sure that all parties to the contract will be in attendance. Then, when you show up with your offer, his wife had better be there or they will have to face your wrath. "I know I was very specific when I called, and you assured me that your wife would be home," you storm. "I simply don't have the time to make five trips back and forth, and to tell the truth, I am very disappointed. I'll tell you what. I offered $50,000 for the house, and I'll leave that open until eleven tomorrow morning. But if you wait beyond that, my offer will drop to $49,000."

Never say anything you don't mean. At the bottom of the offer there will be a space for limiting the time of acceptance. Write, "Offer good until 11:00 A.M., (tomorrow's date)." And if the offer has not been accepted, rewrite it with the new price of $49,000. They will get the message immediately.

I don't want to seem to be advocating that you play a rough game with innocent sellers. But if you ask that every interested party be present when the offer is presented, you can eliminate the dangers inherent in the "invisible partner" tactic.

Time is an important element in acceptance. I never allow sellers a day or two to consider objections and prepare a counter offer. Do you think they will make a counter offer that will insist you pay *less* than your original offer? Of course not; if they make a counter offer, they will be demanding concessions on your part. But if you insist on immediate acceptance, they are put in a position in which they must either accept your offer, modify it on the spot (and face-to-face), or reject it altogether. In any case, you remain in control.

Find out all you can about the sellers.

1. *Why are they selling?* Probably the most important question. The best deals are always those in which the seller must sell right away. If they are just advertising the house "to see what someone would pay for it," they are only wasting your time. But if, as in a recent case I ran into, the husband has been transferred to another state and the wife is still at home, trying desperately to sell, then you have the makings of a perfect deal.

2. *How much do they want as a down payment and what are they going to do with the money?* This is another question I always ask. The reason for asking this question is simply to ensure that they really *need* that money. We've already discussed needs versus wants. With this question you can find out if they really *need* that $20,000 in cash.

Armed with a knowledge of the sellers' needs and motivation for selling, you will find that negotiating becomes a much easier chore.

Start with small talk.

Don't jump into a negotiation head first. Start with small talk, especially as you walk around the house together. Talk about common interests, family, hobbies, etc. Establish rapport. There are two good reasons for this: First, you will be "breaking the ice," freeing up the conversational floes that would otherwise block open communication. Second, by spending a little time getting to know the other person, you will have time pressure and social pressure working in your favor. It's much more difficult to turn someone down and walk away from the table when you feel a social bond, no matter how slight. You will be giving yourself to the other party as well, but if you recognize that fact you shouldn't have difficulty staying in control of the negotiation.

I was recently able to combine several of the negotiating

strategies mentioned so far, and the result was another excellent deal.

I made an offer on a home in which the owners had $60,000 equity. They wanted every penny of that equity in cash . . . but that's not what they *needed*. I talked them into accepting $24,000 down and taking the other $36,000 in payments, but the down payment was still too high for me, so I kept talking. They insisted that they needed at least $24,000 in cash, and it looked like I was going to miss out on the transaction.

Unwilling to give up, and seeking common ground, I looked around the room. On the bookcase were several gymnastic trophies, and since my own daughter was involved in gymnastics we started talking about how well their daughter had done. And, lo and behold, who should walk in but their daughter. We talked, and she informed me that she was a senior in high school. She would be going to college the following year, and when she mentioned the university I told her the tuition was very expensive. She said, "It sure is; it will cost $6,000 a year just for tuition."

Now I knew the sellers' needs: They *needed* $6,000 a year for four years. I restructured the terms of my offer, and they accepted it. What do you suppose I offered? Of course: $6,000 per year for four years, with no interest, and the remaining $36,000 at a low interest rate. My initial down payment was only $6,000 on an $85,000 house.

All sellers want cash. Few sellers, however, truly need all of their equity in cash, and the few that do probably aren't the deals you are looking for anyway. Talk to the sellers face-to-face, and *find out their needs, not wants.*

Present yourself well.

Look at it from the sellers' viewpoint. What does the seller see when you knock on the door and look at his or her property? First impressions are very important. Picture this: You are trying to sell your home, and a prospective buyer appears at the door, offer in hand. You fail to notice the spaghetti stains on his T-shirt because they are obliterated by the grease marks. The tennis shoes are definitely on their last laces, and you would suspect his socks would be in the same state—if he was wearing any.

Do I need to go on, or do you have the picture? This gentleman may have a million dollars socked away in a bank account, but you aren't likely to finance him for ten cents. Of course, my example is extreme, but it makes a point often overlooked by prospective buyers. If you are going to ask sellers to lend you $10,000, you had better convince them that you are a good risk. Wear a sharp-looking outfit. A tux or evening gown is going a bit far, but a tie or even a nice suit isn't out of place. Most people will be happy to lend you anything you need . . . as long as you look like you don't need it.

The second suggestion that I have was given to me by a student. He has a short biography that he gives every seller along with his offer. The biography includes not only a brief history, but letters of recommendation from a priest, a banker, and a local politician. He even got his boss to write a letter stating that he is a good employee, that he is honest, loyal, courteous, kind, and a good scout in all other ways as well.

First impressions can't be overestimated. If you convince the sellers that you're a land shark at a feeding frenzy, how amenable do you think they'll be? They'll probably think you eat defenseless sellers for breakfast, lunch, and dinner. Instead, establish an air of mutual trust by getting to know them; by finding out and then being sympathetic to their need to sell. Remember, the best deals in real estate are the result of someone's misfortune. Your duty as an investor isn't to take advantage of problems; it's to solve those problems and make a profit at the same time.

Explain to the sellers that while you understand and sympathize with their plight, you can't be expected to help them out and take a loss at the same time. You should have a plan whereby their problem is solved *and* you can profit. If you can convince them that you have their interests in mind while you invest, they will be willing to work with you.

The *written* offer is the real offer.

This is the last—and perhaps the most important—key to good negotiating in real estate. It's not an uncommon experience for me to have students approach and say, "Mr. Wayner, I've heard you speak several times now and I thoroughly enjoy your lessons." When I ask them how they are doing with their own investments they respond, somewhat embarrassed, "Well, I haven't actually bought any real estate yet, but—" And if I ask them how many written offers they've made, I usually get the same response: "None yet, but—"

The last part of the negotiation is the *written offer*. Look at it this way: If you never make a written offer, you'll never buy any real estate. Common sense should tell you that much. No matter where the conversation at the kitchen table leads, and no matter where it ends, it is meaningless if you don't follow up with a written offer. Later in the book we'll look at that contract in more detail. For now, keep in mind that no negotiation is complete without an offer in writing.

Chapter Six Summary

   I. The first key to negotiating, from the first phone call to the written offer, is finding out the sellers' *needs,* not *wants.* Their asking price will be based on their *wants;* what they will actually accept will be determined by their *needs.*

  II. If you seem to be at an impasse, use one or more of these tactics to reach an agreement:
    A. Concentrate on minor issues. If the price is a problem, back away from it and discuss the down payment or the repairs that need to be done. If you can reach common ground on another point, come back to the price again later.
    B. Trade concessions. Give a little, take a little. For every point you concede, insist that the other party give into one of your demands. If they

want a higher down payment and you can afford it, exchange that for a lower selling price.

C. Use time pressure. Point out how much time has been spent on the negotiations, and show your willingness to back away. The last thing they'll want to do is start negotiations all over again with another potential buyer.

III. Find out all you can about the sellers. Find out why they are selling and how long they have to sell. Don't just ask how much they want for a down payment; find out why they think they need that much. Chances are good they don't *need* nearly as much as they are asking.

IV. Establish rapport by using small talk. Show a genuine interest in the sellers. Find common ground besides the house itself so you can both feel comfortable as you negotiate. Every second spent with them is to your advantage, as it will give you a clearer picture of their needs.

V. Present yourself as anything but a real estate sharpie. Don't whip out the financial calculator and try to impress them with your knowledge of real estate tactics. On the other hand, don't under-impress them either; if they think you're a bumbling idiot, they won't be too eager to hand over the keys to their house. In fact, when we talk about working with bankers in Chapter Seven, I'll give you a few more pointers for proving your credibility to sellers and bankers alike.

VI. If you want to buy real estate, make *written* offers. Coming to a verbal agreement (or failing to come to a verbal agreement) isn't the last step; in fact, the first concrete step in a real estate transaction is when the seller accepts the buyer's written offer. By the time you finish this book, you'll have all the information you need to make a written offer. *Use* that information!

Chapter Six Homework

1. If you've done your homework so far, you should be ready to begin negotiating with sellers. Find at least one possible deal and begin preliminary negotiations, using the strategies outlined in this chapter. If you don't feel ready to commit yourself, or if the deal falls through, make a list of things that went wrong and how you can improve your performance in the future.

2. Call a seller from a classified ad tonight. Find out the seller's needs and at least attempt to begin the negotiating over the phone. If the deal sounds interesting, follow it up by making an appointment to see the property this week.

Part Three

Structure the Deal

Chapter Seven

Real Estate Finance

This is the toughest chapter in the book. Real estate finance can be hard to understand because it involves **borrowed money.** It's not the borrowing that's confusing; it's the repaying.

Paying for Dirt

Understand first that because of its high cost, real estate is almost always purchased with borrowed funds. Because of this, the lender will want some return on his investment. That is, he isn't going to give the borrower free money. Makes sense, right?

So we can break the purchase into two parts: the down payment and the **loan.** The down payment we can dispense with quickly; in most cases (and we'll talk about exceptions shortly) it must be paid in cash, out of the buyer's pocket.

To understand how the loan works, we'll have to look at four factors: the **principal,** the **interest,** the **payments,** and the **term** of the loan.

The amount borrowed is called the principal. It must be repaid some time during the term of the loan, in any manner agreed upon between the borrower and lender. The interest is a percentage charged by the lender for the use of its money. The payments, obviously, are how the repayment is made. The loan may call for equal payments, for graduated payments, for a lump-sum payment at the end of the term, or any combination of the above. The term is the length of time specified by the lender for repayment.

Amortization

The most important concept to understand in finance is amortization. The word amortization comes from a Latin word, amort, which means "death." Literally translated, as a loan is amortized it is killed off; and that's not a bad translation because that's exactly what happens. Mostly the word is nice and official sounding. Professionals, such as real estate lawyers and bankers, couldn't very well go around wearing official-looking suits and official-looking expressions and then say something like, "This loan'll be killed off in thirty years." But we can say, "This loan will be fully amortized over a thirty-year term."

If I lend you $100 and you promise to pay me $10 per month for the next ten months, the loan will be fully amortized. Pretty simple, huh? Now what if you want to pay it off over a period of one year? Well, we'll divide the $100 by 12 (months), and you will owe me $8.33 every month except the last, when you'll have to pay $8.37. Now, to make it just a tiny bit complicated, I'll insist that you pay me 12 percent interest on the full amount, for a total repayment of $112. Dividing again by 12, you will owe me $9.33 per month.

We don't really have a problem until you take two years to pay me back. Then I will want you to pay me 12 percent *per year* on the unpaid balance. In fact, I will divide that 12 percent annual rate by 12, charging you 1 percent every month on the unpaid balance. How can we figure out a payment plan whereby you can pay off the loan with 24 monthly installments always paying interest on the unpaid balance and yet killing off the loan perfectly in two years?

Let's jump ahead a little. Suppose I lend you $80,000 at 12 percent interest for thirty years. How in the world can we determine a monthly payment that will allow you to always pay your interest on the unpaid balance plus a portion of the principal, until, at the end of thirty years, *voilà!* the entire loan has been fully amortized?

(If you have had enough experience with finance to know what I'm leading up to—figuring out amortization formulas— you are no doubt thinking, "Boy, Steve, have you painted yourself into a corner! I took two years of that stuff in college and never did understand it." Just watch this.)

You don't ever need to know how it was figured out, but somebody did come up with a formula (you don't even want to see it, trust me), and it works. All you have to do is feed the amount of the loan, the interest rate, and the term of the loan into the formula and it will give you the answer. You really don't have to understand how the formula works to use it, any more than you need to understand how a car engine works to drive.

Today you can buy a financial calculator (every investor should have one) for under thirty dollars which will fully amortize a loan for you and calculate your monthly payments. The computer I'm using to write these words with can calculate an amortization schedule (a schedule of payments) for me in about ten seconds.

Each payment will include a portion of principal and a portion of interest. It's easy to see that at first the interest will comprise most of the payment because it is always charged on the unpaid balance of the principal, and the principal is still quite large. Toward the end of the amortization (the payment schedule) the principal is almost completely paid off, so the interest portion of the payment is almost nonexistent.

An example of an amortization schedule based on the $80,000, thirty-year loan at 12 percent is shown on page 162.

LOAN AMORTIZATION SCHEDULE

ORDER NO.		PRINCIPAL AMOUNT	INTEREST RATE	PAYMENT	NO. OF PAYMENTS
92748 35	360	$ 80,000.00	12.00000	822.89	360 PAYMENTS MONTHLY

NO	PAYMENT	INTEREST	PRINCIPAL	BALANCE
1	822.89	800.00	22.89	79,977.11
2	822.89	799.77	23.12	79,953.99
3	822.89	799.54	23.35	79,930.64
4	822.89	799.31	23.58	79,907.06
5	822.89	799.07	23.82	79,883.24
6	822.89	798.83	24.06	79,859.18
7	822.89	798.59	24.30	79,834.88
8	822.89	798.35	24.54	79,810.34
9	822.89	798.10	24.79	79,785.55
10	822.89	797.86	25.03	79,760.52
11	822.89	797.61	25.28	79,735.24
12	822.89	797.35	25.54	79,709.70
13	822.89	797.10	25.79	79,683.91
14	822.89	796.84	26.05	79,657.86
15	822.89	796.58	26.31	79,631.55
16	822.89	796.32	26.57	79,604.98
17	822.89	796.05	26.84	79,578.14
18	822.89	795.78	27.11	79,551.03
19	822.89	795.51	27.38	79,523.65
20	822.89	795.24	27.65	79,496.00
21	822.89	794.96	27.93	79,468.07
22	822.89	794.68	28.21	79,439.86
23	822.89	794.40	28.49	79,411.37
24	822.89	794.11	28.78	79,382.59
25	822.89	793.83	29.06	79,353.53
26	822.89	793.54	29.35	79,324.18
27	822.89	793.24	29.65	79,294.53
28	822.89	792.95	29.94	79,264.59
29	822.89	792.65	30.24	79,234.35
30	822.89	792.34	30.55	79,203.80
31	822.89	792.04	30.85	79,172.95
32	822.89	791.73	31.16	79,141.79
33	822.89	791.42	31.47	79,110.32
34	822.89	791.10	31.79	79,078.53
35	822.89	790.79	32.10	79,046.43
36	822.89	790.46	32.43	79,014.00
37	822.89	790.14	32.75	78,981.25
38	822.89	789.81	33.08	78,948.17
39	822.89	789.48	33.41	78,914.76
40	822.89	789.15	33.74	78,881.02
41	822.89	788.81	34.08	78,846.94
42	822.89	788.47	34.42	78,812.52
43	822.89	788.13	34.76	78,777.76
44	822.89	787.78	35.11	78,742.65
45	822.89	787.43	35.46	78,707.19
46	822.89	787.07	35.82	78,671.37
47	822.89	786.71	36.18	78,635.19
48	822.89	786.35	36.54	78,598.65
49	822.89	785.99	36.90	78,561.75
50	822.89	785.62	37.27	78,524.48
51	822.89	785.24	37.65	78,486.83
52	822.89	784.87	38.02	78,448.81
348	822.89	784.49		78,410.41
349	822.89		730.26	8,…
350	822.89	85.33	737.56	7,795.25
351	822.89	77.95	744.94	7,050.31
352	822.89	70.50	752.39	6,297.92
353	822.89	62.98	759.91	5,538.01
354	822.89	55.38	767.51	4,770.50
355	822.89	47.71	775.18	3,995.32
356	822.89	39.95	782.94	3,212.38
357	822.89	32.12	790.77	2,421.61
358	822.89	24.22	798.67	1,622.94
359	822.89	16.23	806.66	816.28
360	824.44	8.16	816.28	0.00
TOTAL INTEREST	216,241.95			

That's the rudiments of how amortization works. You can see that because you are always paying the interest on the unpaid balance, the beginning payments are almost exclusively interest. But as the principal balance declines, the interest declines also, so that by the end of the term your payments are almost completely principal.

And that was enough for many years. But after the turbulent '70s, escalating prices and rising interest rates made long-term loans with fixed interest rates unprofitable for bankers and made monthly payments too high for home buyers. For example, in 1976 you might have found a loan for $60,000 with an interest rate of 12 percent. On a thirty-year term your payments would have been $617.17. But only a couple of years later you would probably have needed $76,000 or so for the same home, and you would have been lucky to find a loan that only carried a 15.5 percent interest rate. Your payment would have soared to $991.43, a difference of $374.26. Wages didn't keep up with housing, so new borrowers became scarce. And banks were forced to find new ways to amortize loans.

Today we have some loans, such as *graduated payment mortgages,* in which there is **negative amortization** in the first few years of the loan. What that means is that the payments are so low that they don't even cover the interest charge. As a result, the borrower actually owes more at the end of the year than at the beginning! In fact, with negative amortization you are charged interest on interest. The entire loan is paid off by the end of the term, but you end up paying more in the later years of the loan than you would have if the payments had been level.

With a **balloon mortgage,** a schedule will often be worked out like the preceding one, with payments figured on a thirty-year term, but after a period of time (ten years is common) the remaining balance would be due in one large payment.

As you learn more complicated finance techniques, you will find that loans can be "killed off" in as many ways as your creativity will allow. I've seen some loans that are negatively amortized for the first ten years, and then level payments for the next ten years, followed by accelerated amortization the last ten years to make up for the negative amortization the first ten years! When you are going to an institutional lender for a loan, have the loan officer explain how it will be amortized. If you don't understand the explanations, back up and have it explained more thoroughly.

Here is one of the best negotiating tips I can give you, but it had to wait for this chapter: If you are trying to convince a seller to let you pay him for his equity in equal payments (seller financing), prepare an amortization schedule in advance and attach it to the offer. Often, when the interest income is added up and laid out in black and white, many sellers are persuaded to take payments instead of all cash for their equity.

That should be a good start on the concept of amortization and repaying borrowed money. One of your homework problems will be to buy and then learn to use a financial calculator. After a few practice sessions working with the instruction book, you'll feel comfortable pulling out your HP-12C (Hewlett-Packard's popular financial calculator) and figuring payments on any loan imaginable.

If you don't want to invest in a calculator right now, but want to figure out amortization schedules, I will send you an amortization card for free. Send $1 to cover postage and handling to me at P.O. Box 562047, Miami, Florida 33256.

The Down Payment

As I mentioned earlier, you'll have two obligations when you buy real estate. One is the loan, and we'll cover getting a new loan and assuming existing loans later in this chapter. The second part is the down payment, and that's the one that seems to trip up most investors. The sellers all seem to want cash, and the buyers don't want to part with one more penny that they absolutely have to.

That simple problem has caused more trouble than any other. Buyers for some reason, seem to feel they have no options other than to pay that hated down payment in cash—their own cash—and that can mean tens of thousands of dollars at closing.

If you don't have the required down payment gathering dust in your savings account, you actually have five options: You can borrow the money (find a partner); you can negotiate a nothing-down deal; you can use an alternative to cash; you can offer sweat equity; or you can give up investing.

Let's throw the fifth option out right now. You are reading this book for a specific reason: to learn how to buy real estate. *You* aren't going to let a little thing like no money stop you from succeeding, are you? Of course not! So let's look at each of the other four choices.

Borrow. If you don't have the money, somebody else does—bet on it. If you have a friend or relative with money, that is often the best place to go for a loan. If not, try finding someone in your community with extra cash. Banks may lend you the money, but it is rather unlikely that any bank will be willing to lend you money to buy real estate when you cannot afford the down payment. And if they are kind enough to part with some of their hard-earned money, you will probably have to pay an arm and a leg, sign in blood, sell your soul, and leave your mother-in-law as collateral.

Borrowing money from those who have it isn't as tough as it sounds—if you've done your homework. Find the deal, structure the terms, make a definite long-range plan, type everything up on paper, and *then* go looking for a partner. Offer your partner every penny of his or her investment back within one year plus a share of the profit.

This is such an excellent way to get started that I am going to take a minute and spell it out for you in more detail. Suppose you have found a nice little house that is worth at least $75,000. The seller has been transferred out of state and is a little desperate—he has been trying to sell it long distance for three months now, and the payments are getting seriously painful. The yard is overrun with dying weeds and the general appearance, inside and out, is, well . . . seedy. Nobody seems to be interested in buying and he can't take care of it himself. He is willing to let you assume his $53,000 mortgage if you will give him $5,000 cash for his equity. That's right: You can buy this house for $58,000. (Don't laugh—this is an actual case.)

You know you can sell the house easily for $70,000 after investing one or two Saturdays fixing up the place. It doesn't need much; a lawn mower and a hose would take care of a lot of the problem. And your payments will be $550 a month; not bad, considering that such a home will rent for $625 or more.

You don't know anyone with an extra $5,000 to spare, and you blew your savings last night at Burger King. No problem. No problem? That's right; no problem at all—it's only a matter of perspective. What you need is a convincing letter that you can send to about a hundred potential partners. Doctors, lawyers, dentists, plumbers . . . anyone who makes a lot of money is someone whose life you can enrich with this excellent deal.

Your plan is as follows: You will purchase the house, using your partner's money and doing the fix-up yourself. The house will be rented for at least one year and will then be sold for at least $72,000. When it is sold, you will return your partner's money to him or her and the remaining equity will be divided equally. Furthermore, any tax advantages of ownership (depreciation) will be given to your partner. (Well, if you can barely afford dinner at Burger King, you aren't in a tax bracket high enough to worry about it.) Quick now: How much will your return be, expressed as a percentage, and how much will your partner make on his or her investment? Let's figure it out together:

Purchase price	$58,000
Selling price	72,000
Profit	14,000
Less partner's investment	5,000
Equity to be split	$9,000

You can see that each of you will receive $4,500 after your partner takes $5,000 off the top. Going back to my question, what is your return? Well, if it was somebody else's money that was used, and not one dime left your pocket, your return cannot be calculated; it approaches infinity! And don't think I have forgotten about the rental income. You were making—and keeping—$75 a month for one year, which is $900. Add that to your $4,500 profit and you get a total of $5,400. Your partner has a deduction for depreciation, plus the original investment of $5,000, plus $4,500 profit. All in all it's a real Win/Win situation, and you are on the road to financial freedom.

Contacting possible partners may seem to be a formidable task, but you don't actually have to approach them face-to-face if it makes you uncomfortable. A form letter can be sent to every professional in your community, and if you have a computer like the one I'm looking at right now, it can insert their names and addresses, making it more personal. Your letter should be brief and to the point. Introduce yourself and outline the proposal. Give them your name and address so they can contact you if they are interested. This is a shotgun approach, but if your letter is well planned and the proposal financially seductive enough, a hundred letters should turn up at least a handful of interested parties. And all you need is *one*.

I don't know yet why this is such a difficult concept for new investors, unless they just aren't sure enough of themselves. Every time I use an example like the one above in a seminar and ask for a show of hands from people who have the funds to back such a deal—and who would gladly form such a partnership—I get a strong response. If you brought me such a deal and convinced me you knew what you were talking about, I would gladly back your investment. Look at it from your partner's point of view, and use your own common sense.

Let's move on to your second option: **Negotiate a nothing-down deal.** When you find out how much the seller wants as a down payment and *why* he or she wants the money, you will know what your chances are of negotiating such a deal. Ordinarily, sellers really do need at least part of their equity in cash, but there are certainly instances where sellers really don't need anything at all. In the example given above, the seller had been transferred and had already bought a house; he really didn't need $10,000 to put down on a new home. It is possible that you could have convinced him to take all of his equity in payments.

Another possibility is offering a higher price than the seller is asking in exchange for a nothing-down deal. If, in the previous example, the buyer had offered to pay $65,000 instead of $58,000, the additional $7,000 might have been temptation enough to convince the seller to take back a second mortgage. And you could still have fixed up and sold the house within a couple of months for $70,000 or more. The trade-off is obvious: By raising the price to create a nothing-down deal, you are saddling yourself with much higher monthly payments, which may destroy your positive cash flow and possibly cause a severe financial headache if you can't sell the house as easily as you had anticipated. For that reason I suggest you approach this option very carefully. The partnership idea will usually be more advantageous and much safer.

Besides, I think you should concentrate your efforts in learning your market area and putting together a few good deals that might require something as a down payment. Nothing-down deals are great, *when* you find them and *when* they will lead to either positive rental cash flow or a profitable sale. But it isn't easy, and if you insist on buying only nothing-down properties, rather than coming up with creative methods for acquiring the necessary down payment, you will be severely restricting your investing career. It's like standing too close to a painting, with your nose pressed against one small detail. Step back and look at the whole picture; there's more than one way to invest successfully in real estate.

Next on the list: **cash alternatives.** I have heard of some incredible down payments. Anything of value is fair game: cars, jewelry, coins, stamps, stocks and bonds. If you own a hamburger stand and the seller loves hamburgers, why not offer a year's worth of hamburgers? The seller wins because he or she is only paying for the hamburgers with equity, which was probably a by-product of inflation. And you win because you pay wholesale for the meat, but you'll get retail value toward your down payment.

Last on the list is **sweat equity,** a dainty little term that means working for your down payment. Returning again to our example, if the house and yard are in poor shape offer to clean them up within a certain period of time as part—or all—of the down payment. You were going to do it anyway, so why not?

Why would the seller be willing to allow you to pay him with your sweat? Because he knows that there is a chance that you will fail to make your payments, and if you do he will have to take back the house. If he cannot take care of the property himself, and if he is having a hard time selling it now because of its condition, he will be happy to have you do all the work and then lose the house back to him. He wins either way: If you do make the payments, he will be receiving that money every month over the life of the contract. If you clean the place up and then fail to make the payments, he can take it back and resell it—at a price much closer to its true market value. And if you make the payments but fail to take care of the clean-up, he still doesn't really lose because you have been making his payments during that month or two.

A combination of each of these suggestions would reduce even a high down payment to nothing at all. It takes courage, effort, creativity, and a belief in yourself (like the little train that could). But it can be done.

Don't let the fact that you have no money for a down payment stop you from investing. Go ahead; look for the good deals in real estate. They are out there waiting for you. If you don't have any money, *somebody* does.

Keeping the Down Payment Low

There is a balance between the size of the down payment and the size of the monthly payments. The higher the down payment, the lower the balance that must be financed, and therefore the lower the monthly payments will be. However, even if you can afford a large down payment, there are several good reasons for keeping it as low as possible.

There are only two exceptions to the low down-payment rule: First, if the seller will discount the selling price considerably in exchange for a larger down payment, you may be able to get a larger return on your investment when you sell. Second, in a case where you want a steady monthly rental cash flow and have no intention of reselling the property, if you can afford the larger down payment, you will be able to generate a monthly return on your investment that will pay handsomely over the years and build up equity.

There is an old joke in the real estate investing world:

"I've got good news and bad news."

"What's the good news?"

"They will sell us the Empire State Building for only two million dollars at 10 percent interest."

"That is great! What's the bad news?"

"They want $500 down."

If you are at all serious about investing, you probably don't want to put *anything* down if you can help it. Even if you can get away with $2,000 down every time, sooner or later you will run out of cash. On the other hand, if you buy one hundred properties with nothing down, but they are all alligators, you will also run out of cash quickly.

Just because you can afford a large down payment doesn't mean you should offer one. There are two good reasons for trying to keep the down payment as low as possible. First, at the time of the printing of this book interest payments on a mortgage are tax deductible, so it would be better putting a small payment down, using the money to feed the alligator each month, and getting most of it back at the end of the year.

For an example we will buy a $60,000 house which will rent for $550 per month. First let's look at the numbers when we put $12,000 down (20%), and then when we put $3,000 down (5%).

I. $12,000 down, thirty-year loan for $48,000 at 12 percent:
monthly payments: $493.73
monthly rental income: 550.00

cash flow: $56.27 \times 12 = \$675.24$ (positive)

II. $3,000 down, thirty-year loan for $57,000 at 12 percent:
monthly payments: $586.31
monthly rental income: <u>550.00</u>
cash flow: $-36.31 \times 12 = -$435.72
                                 (alligator!)

The difference in your annual return is $1,110.96 . . . before taxes. However, for at least the first few years almost the entire difference is in interest payments, which may be tax deductible. New tax proposals may limit the amount of the interest deduction. Check with your CPA for details. Furthermore, if you had $12,000 to put down but only used $3,000 of it, you are left with $9,000, which will cover your negative cash flow for about ten years if you keep it in the bank earning interest.

The second reason for using a small down payment is that it will be so much easier to get that money back out of the property when you sell it. We'll use the same example and assume that you can sell the property immediately. In the situation above you are much more likely to be able to sell the property for $63,000 with $6,000 down (recovering your $3,000 investment and making a $3,000 cash profit) than for $63,000 with $15,000 down (to make the same $3,000 cash profit). And if you do sell it for $63,000 in either case, here is the immediate return on your investment:

I. investment: $12,000
profit: 3,000
profit, as a percentage return on investment: 25%

Not a bad return, *if* you can find someone to give you the full $12,000 down. But it is so much better in the second case:

II. investment: $3,000
profit: 3,000
profit, as a percentage return on investment: 100%

Much, much better; you are doubling your money. And it is very likely that you can find a buyer willing to give you $6,000 down, cashing you out entirely so you can realize your profit instantly.

The down payment can always be negotiated to death, until you arrive at the very lowest *need* of the seller—and can satisfy that need. Then it's up to you: Form a partnership with someone who has it; work for it; use a cash substitute; or walk away and wait for an even better deal.

Getting a Loan

You've worked out half the problem—the down payment. Now it's time for the other half—the loan. If you have $60,000 socked away in the bank, you might want to pay cash—you can get tremendous discounts for cash. However, few of us have that kind of greenery decorating our accounts, and that means getting the money from someone else. There are at least four sources of funds: the seller, a conventional lender, the government, or a private investor.

Borrowing from the Seller

We've already spent quite a bit of time discussing this, and yet many people fail to recognize the seller as the greatest source of real estate financing. Sellers can help you in two ways: They can lend you their equity, by accepting monthly payments; and they can allow you to assume their existing loans.

As a recap on the idea of borrowing the seller's equity: Attach an amortization schedule to your offers, showing the sellers how much more they would receive in interest income by accepting payments. Convince them that by making payments you can afford to buy their properties, thereby eliminating their problem. Possibly offer a higher purchase price in exchange for a smaller down payment (if the deal will still be profitable). Never forget Steven Wayner's Golden Rule of real estate investing: "Thou shalt always have a positive cash flow."

Assuming the Loan

When a buyer gets a new loan from the bank (or any lending institution), it is either "assumable" or "nonassumable." If the owner sells the house and the loan is *fully assumable,* the new buyer may assume the obligation (make the payments) and the loan is transferred to the new owner without any changes. If it is *nonassumable* it may not be transferred, and the new owner must find new financing.

The extent of the difference has become especially apparent in the last few years, as interest rates have roller-coastered their way through the '70s and '80s. Where rates will be next month—or even next week—seems to be anyone's guess. Not long ago lenders felt comfortable making loans as low as 8 or 9 percent, never dreaming what would happen to interest rates. And, of course, those loans were fully assumable.

To understand the amazing effect the rate has on the payment, compare a thirty-year loan for $50,000 at different interest rates:

Rate	Monthly Payment
9.0	$402.31
9.5	420.43
10.0	438.79
10.5	457.37
11.0	476.16
11.5	495.15
12.0	514.31
12.5	533.63
13.0	553.10
13.5	572.71
14.0	592.44
14.5	612.28
15.0	632.22
15.5	652.26
16.0	672.38

I don't suppose I have to stress the difference between a monthly payment of $402 and $672. But that is the difference between finding an assumable loan at 9 percent and having to secure a new loan at 16 percent. With the volatile price of money—that's what the interest rate is: the price of money—it is easy to understand why assumable loans are a vanished breed, and the few assumable loans you can find below current rates should *always* be assumed.

The Due-on-Sale Clause

I think the due-on-sale clause is perhaps the single most destructive thing ever to happen in real estate finance. Another similar clause is called an acceleration clause, and it operates in much the same way. In either case, the person who has a mortgage with this odious clause in it cannot transfer his title to a buyer without the lender's approval. If he attempts to do so, the lender can call the entire amount due (hence the name).

Because these clauses prevent a simple assumption of the loan, buyers are forced to either assume them formally, paying the lender several points *and* having a higher interest rate on the loan, or to find a new loan, giving up the old loan entirely. Before 1978, conventional loans were usually assumable without a hike in the interest rate. But as interest rates began to get out of control, banks found that they had outstanding loans that they were earning 10 percent or less on, while they were forced to pay even higher rates on deposits. Their profits shrank and threatened to disappear altogether. To combat those losses they came up with clauses that stipulated that if the loan was ever assumed the interest rate would rise to current levels. No more 10 percent loans were going to be shuffled from seller to buyer; no sir! From then on, every time a piece of property was sold and a loan assumed, that interest rate was going to jump up to where it belonged.

The banks may have had a good point from their own perspective, but it's easy to see the effect it had on investors. With interest rates so high it was the assumption of low interest rate loans that allowed them to invest. The due-on-sale clause hampered buyers and sellers, causing a massive slowdown in home sales.

If you are considering assuming a loan, find out if it contains an acceleration or a due-on-sale clause. If the seller isn't sure, check with the lender or have an attorney read the loan documentation. There are entire books and study courses devoted to avoiding the due-on-sale clause. For further information, contact Jodestar Seminars, P.O. Box 562047, Miami, Florida 33256.

VA (Veteran's Administration) and most FHA (Federal Housing Administration) loans are usually assumable (that is, they do not contain a due-on-sale clause), and many pre-1978 conventional loans are assumable as well. *Always* ask the seller when you call if the loan is assumable and, if so, what the interest rate is.

Even if the loan is assumable, lenders have different requirements for the assumption. Some loans are assumable, but you must requalify; others, such as FHA and VA, can be taken over with a **simple assumption**, and you don't have to qualify for the loan at all to assume it—you cannot be turned down. Many loans can only be assumed by owner-occupants. However, effective January 1, 1987, all new FHA loans are nonassumable the first two years of the loan. If you want to buy it as a rental property, you will have to get a new loan.

The way to find out in every case is to ask the owner who the lender is. Then you can call the lender and ask about assuming the loan. They can tell you what restrictions apply, if any, and what applications must be filled out. They will also be happy to tell you how much you will owe them for letting you assume the loan. If the loan requires a **formal assumption**, there may be a large fee, you will have to qualify for the loan yourself, and the interest rate may go up. That's why I so strongly recommend that you keep your eyes open for the assumable FHA and VA loans.

If you find an assumable loan and the interest rate is lower than current rates, you should assume it—after you have found out all you can about it. Most of the information you'll need should be a matter of asking common-sense questions, such as "Who do I make the payments to?" In addition, however, there may be a few questions that won't occur to you until after you have assumed the loan. Let me give you a list of questions that you should always ask—and don't be afraid to ask anything else you can think of.

> How much are the monthly payments? Does that include taxes and insurance?
>
> Do the payments change each month, or each year, or are they fixed?
>
> Do the payments increase if the taxes or insurance increase?
>
> What is the interest rate on the loan? Does it change, or is it permanently fixed?
>
> If the interest rate does change, under what circumstances will it do so?
>
> If it changes, how often will it do so, and how much can it change; is there a limit (a cap)?
>
> Do I have the right to prepay the mortgage without a prepayment penalty?
>
> Is there an escrow (impound) account? If there is, what fees are held in the account (taxes, insurance, waste collection)?
>
> Is there an escalation (due-on-sale clause?) (This question is very important, if there is a due-on-sale clause you may not be able to assume the loan at all.)
>
> Is there a transfer fee? If there is, how much is it?
>
> What is the charge if the payment is late, and how many days is the grace period?

Every one of these questions will help you make a decision about assuming an existing mortgage. Don't be afraid to ask any other question you can think of. If you think knowing the owner's shoe size will help you, by all means ask; it's the unasked question that always gets you into trouble later.

If you have a choice between assuming an existing loan and getting a new loan at the same rate, which would you choose? Take a minute and figure it out.

I would always rather assume the existing loan. Why? Because it will still be assumable when I sell the property; a new loan may or may not be assumable. If I keep the property for six months and interest rates climb to the top of Mt. Everest in the meantime, I'm not going to be able to offer my buyer the lower rate—unless I've had the foresight to assume the old loan. Remember to watch your long-range plan as you make decisions!

FHA & VA Loans

In the last section I mentioned two particular types of loans that at present are fully assumable: FHA and VA loans. An explanation of each is in order.

The Federal Housing Authority was established during the Great Depression to help cure the ailing housing market with new loan guarantees. The FHA would guarantee repayment of a low-interest, long-term loan made by a conventional lender. In exchange for the guarantee, the borrower would only have to pay an additional 1/2 percent on the loan.

Today the FHA has been dissolved into the Department of Housing and Urban Development (HUD), so in reality there is no Federal Housing Authority. However, FHA loans are still available, so the name remains.

The wonderful advantage of these loans to investors is that they are fully assumable. If the seller has an FHA loan on his house, you can assume that loan without restriction. You *cannot* be turned down by the lender, and the interest rate cannot be increased. Not only that, but the fee for assuming an FHA loan is presently $45, plus a small loan statement fee. Not only do you save thousands of dollars when you buy, but when you're ready to sell you can advertise your fully assumable FHA loan and attract buyers—especially investors—like a newly washed car attracts rain clouds.

Looking through the newspaper you will occasionally come across a classified ad that offers a low-interest FHA loan. Call immediately! These loans are an investor's dream come true. (Remember, all FHA loans taken out after January 1, 1987, cannot be assumed for the first two years of the loan!)

VA is the acronym for the Veterans Administration, a government program that was set up to assist veterans. A VA loan is not a loan offered by the Veterans Administration; rather, it is a conventional (bank) loan on which the VA guarantees payment. If the veteran ever defaults on the loan, the VA promises to buy the mortgage from the lender and then foreclose in its own name.

It seems to be an ideal arrangement. The banks are very willing to make the loan because they will get their money whether or not the payments are made. The veteran, through the generosity of Uncle Sam (that's you and me), is able to buy a home with little or no down payment at a lower interest rate. And Uncle Sam (us again) is so rich that even if the loan is defaulted on, he will hardly notice the extra burden of debt. After all, when you're in debt for over a trillion dollars, what's another $60,000?

If you are a veteran you are probably already aware of the VA loan; if you weren't before, you are now. Consider it as a way of buying your first home. But what if you're not a veteran? Well, I have wonderful news: A VA loan can be assumed by *anyone*. It's been said—with justification—that if a mirror fogs up when held under your nose, you are qualified to assume a VA loan. The cost to assume the loan? Presently $45! And there is no due-on-sale clause or escalation clause to stop you; you take over the loan immediately, with no changes in its terms whatsoever.

There is a danger in the assumption of a VA loan to the veteran. If the loan is assumed and then subsequently defaulted on, the original borrower—the veteran—is held personally liable to the VA for the loan. If you are a veteran and have a VA loan, screen prospective buyers carefully or don't allow them to assume your loan.

When the VA repossesses a property, it is offered for sale to the public through approved real estate brokers. To get a list of VA repossessions, ask any broker in your area. The list will include the address, the asking price, and the down payment, and of the three, only the address is not subject to negotiation. The agent you contact will have a key to the lockbox on the door of the house and can show you through it. If you determine that the asking price is good, you can make an offer, which will be submitted to a review board.

When competition for VA repos is tight, you are unlikely to get any fantastic deals. The VA considers each bid separately, giving first priority to owner-occupants (as opposed to investors), then to price, and then to terms. A standard rule in such cases is to offer at least 3 percent more, plus a few dollars, than the VA is asking. If the price is still in the right range, you may find yourself with a new property.

Occasionally there will be a glut of new VA repos, especially during times of high unemployment. The market will be slow and houses won't be selling. That's the best time to bid on these properties. You can offer less than the asking price, and only 5 percent down, and get an extraordinary bargain.

There are a couple more advantages to buying VA repos. The sales commission is paid to the broker by the VA, so there is no price increase to cover that expense. And the VA claims to have good title to the property, so they will not expect you to get title insurance.

When you are reading the classified ads, looking for houses to buy, watch closely for "assumable VA loan."

Creative Finance

Before we move on to conventional means of financing (approaching a loan officer on your hands and knees, holding your first-born out before you), let's stop and consider the term "creative finance."

It may be a difficult concept to grasp, but you and the seller can arrange *any* kind of financing imaginable—as long as it's legal. Let someone else worry about putting it into legalese; just come to an agreement. Try to look beyond conventional finance techniques. Get creative!

Toward the end of the chapter we'll take a look at several creative techniques for financing your purchases. As you become more familiar with the terrain of real estate finance, you'll be able to come up with your own ideas. Don't be afraid to think creatively; you're only restricted by your own imagination.

Conventional Financing

If the seller can't finance all of the sale, either through a personal loan or through an assumption, you'll probably have to turn to conventional means for the money: a bank, a mortgage company, or a savings and loan. Unfortunately, that means playing by their rules. Fortunately, I can teach you those rules so you can play the game right.

I can't give you a description of current loan programs available through conventional lenders because the loan market is in the midst of upheaval, and by the time you read these words your banker will have a whole slew of new loan programs available.

What I will do is give you a few basics that you can start with, throw some loan lingo at you so you can talk to a banker about ARMs and GPMs with impunity, and try to give you a feel for the ever-changing world of real estate finance.

To understand today's real estate loans we have to go back a few years. Actually, let's go back to the Great Depression. Before that time, real estate loans were made on a yearly basis; the idea of long-term financing was totally unheard of! But when banks failed and unemployment soared, it looked as though everyone in the country would lose their homes. The banks themselves were stuck with thousands of homes they couldn't sell—nobody had the money to buy them. In an effort to bring the housing industry back to life, the federal government created the FHA (Federal Housing Authority), which offered to guarantee home loans. If a banker would give Clyde and Mabel Kadiddlehopper an $8,000 loan, for *20 years,* the FHA would guarantee the loan in case of a default. And to make it even better, the FHA would guarantee a loan of up to 97 percent of the purchase price, leaving Clyde and Mabel to come up with only a $240 down payment! This radical program was totally unheard of, but it was the shot in the arm the housing industry needed, and long-term loans with low down payments caught on. Soon thirty-year loans appeared, and they have been the standard ever since.

The thirty-year fixed rate loan was perfect until the late '70s, when several changes occurred in the money market. First, there was severe inflation, which shocked the nation and left millions of investors shaken. Suddenly dad's advice to put a little money in the bank and earn a solid 5 percent wasn't good enough anymore; people woke up to the fact that they needed to earn as much as possible on their deposits. They pulled the rug out from under the savings and loans, pouring their money into certificates of deposit and money market funds. To compete, the Savings and Loans were forced to offer higher rates on deposits, while at the same time they were collecting payments on the low-interest thirty-year loans. Riding a bucking money market, with interest and inflation rates kicking wildly, many lenders were thrown and some were severly hurt. A handful were forced to close their doors.

But you can't keep a good banker out of the game for long (even if he does seem to lose interest . . .), and lending institutions were quick to come up with loan ideas that would protect their profits. The following are a few brief descriptions of current loan programs:

Adjustable rate mortgage. The ARM was one of the first answers to the bankers' problem. As the name suggests, the interest rate on this loan is *adjustable.* When you apply for the loan you may be paying 12 percent interest, but one year later the interest rate may have jumped to 15 percent.

On a loan of $60,000, a rate increase from 12 percent to

15 percent means a payment increase from $617.17 to $787.71!
Few buyers will survive such a jump. If the loan is for $70,000,
the payments go from an affordable $720.03 to a murderous
$913.16.

The lenders are obviously protected; no matter what happens to interest rates, they can still make money. But for you,
the borrower, borrowing becomes a real poker party. Unless
you are willing to gamble that interest rates won't go up high
enough to force you out of your home, you can't get financing.

To help alleviate the problem—and to attract borrowers
—banks began putting **caps** on their ARMs. A cap is a limit
placed by the lender that prevents the monthly payments from
increasing by more than a given amount each year. If, for example, you got an ARM from the bank with a cap rate of 5
percent, your monthly payments could not rise more than 5 percent each year. In other words, if your payment is $500 this
year, it cannot rise to more than $525 before the end of the
year—no matter what happens to the interest rate. If there was
a 10 percent cap, the payments could rise to $550 this year, but
no more. The peace of mind afforded by these caps swayed
many borrowers to accept the new ARMs, and today they are
common.

Since the interest rate floats, it's important to know what
propels it. Every lender will tie the rate to whatever market
indicator it feels is best. Many ARMs are tied to short-or mid-
term treasury rates. If you are considering an ARM, find out
what index the bank is using; the lender has quite a bit of lee-
way in what index will be used, and some are more volatile
than others.

A few other mortgages offered in the early '80s were of
the same stripe, and they went by such names as VRMs (variable rate mortgages), VIRs (variable interest rate mortgages),
and AMLs (adjustable mortgage loans). But the ARMs proved
to be the most widely accepted, and these loans are by and large
extinct. The few VIRs and VRMs that are still available are
really only slight variations on ARMs.

Graduated payment mortgage. The GPM is another
species of new loan that was created to attract borrowers while

protecting lenders. With the dramatic rise in housing costs, fewer and fewer young couples can afford a house, even in the ranks of upwardly mobile Americans who, a generation ago, would have bought their first home by now.

The payments on a GPM start lower than the payments on a fixed-rate mortgage and rise a little each year. One of the most popular GPMs is made available by the FHA. Payments in the first year are nearly 25 percent less than they would be with a fixed-rate mortgage, and each year they increase 7.5 percent for five years. After that, they remain stable for the life of the mortgage.

There are other GPMs available, and some lenders even combine the GPM with the ARM, coming up with—not surprisingly—the GPM/ARM loan. As I said earlier, I don't want to involve myself too heavily at this point, so I won't attempt to explain how *those* work. However, you shouldn't have any trouble getting a lender to explain his current loan programs if you appear as an interested buyer.

Shared appreciation mortgage. SAMs were more the result of inflation than of skyrocketing interest rates. With inflation came higher prices and enormously high housing prices. Higher prices meant higher payments, and many people simply couldn't afford to make the payment.

With a SAM, the lender agrees to lower the interest rate (and thereby the payment) in exchange for a piece of the profit when the house is sold. For example, the lender may agree to reduce the interest rate from 15 percent to 10 percent, a one-third drop. That's a substantial drop, allowing many new home buyers to move into their first home. In exchange for the lowered rate, however, the lender will receive one-third of the equity when the home is sold.

There is a catch. After ten years (if that is the time period specified by the SAM) if the home is not sold, the balance of the loan is due or the loan must be renegotiated. In either case, the bank claims its portion of the equity at the end of the first ten years, based on an appraisal of the property. If in the above example the house was bought in 1980 for $60,000 and is worth $120,000 in 1990, the bank would claim its one-third share of the appreciation, or $20,000, in addition to the balance of the loan. You can see where there might be a problem with SAMs.

Balloon mortgages. At the end of the term of a mortgage, the principal will either be completely paid off (fully amortized) or there will be a balloon payment due. That's all there is to the idea of a balloon mortgage. In the SAM, there is a balloon payment due at the end of ten years. As an investor you will usually be wise to avoid balloon mortgages, especially if the term of the mortgage is ten years or less. They will be difficult to sell, and if you've ever wanted a decade to pass quickly, just sign on the bottom line. Many people have had balloons burst in their faces.

As an investor, your best bet is to look for assumable mortgages with low interest rates. However, you are narrowing the scope of possible deals if you restrict yourself to the pinch of perfect properties. Instead, learn everything you can about real estate finance; visit your local lenders and ask about their loan programs. Most of them will go out of their way to help you, and the education is free.

Getting a Bank Loan

If you want to get a conventional loan, you will need to make several phone calls; interest rates and terms vary widely. Call the banks and mortgage lenders in your area and ask them what rates they are charging; what different types of loans are available; what their estimated closing costs are; and what kind of prepayment penalty you will be charged if you pay off your loan early.

After you have called several banks, visit those who seemed most willing to work with you and had the best terms available. Sit down with a loan officer and ask the following questions:

Is there always a prepayment penalty? If there is,
can the charge be reduced?

What loan programs are available now, and exactly how does each one work?

Is a new mortgage going to be assumable? (In most cases today, a conventional loan is not assumable, making it more difficult to sell.)

Is there a due-on-sale clause? (Such a clause will force you to pay the loan when you sell the house, which also forces your buyer to find new financing.)

How many points do you charge? (Points are a fee that is charged up front, in cash, to increase the bank's yield on the loan.)

What is your closing cost? (The costs for closing the transaction can be anywhere from $100 to $700 or more, depending on the lending institution.)

What interest rate will you be charging? (The interest rate will vary greatly; some loans will have adjustable rates, others will be fixed rates. The rate is *always* negotiable, and may vary according to how much you can put down on the property.)

You need to shop around for interest rates. Many people have the misconception that all banks and savings and loans charge the same interest rates. That's not true. You can think of lending institutions as money stores—after all, the interest rate is really the price of borrowing money. Does every grocery store charge the same for lettuce? No, there is often a slight difference in price.

To compare interest rates you must take more into consideration than a stated rate. First of all, find out if the rate quoted is the Annual Percentage Rate (APR), which the lender is required by law to give.

Find out how much the loan origination fee will be. This is a fee the lender charges you for being generous enough to lend you its money. It can vary from one lender to the next substantially.

Ask if the rate will be lowered if you make a larger down payment—many banks do offer a discount, because the loan is better secured. Also ask about points. A bank may offer a 12 percent loan with three points, meaning that you will pay 12 percentage points over the term of the loan and three points up front. On a thirty-year fixed-rate loan for $70,000, your payments will be $720.03 and you will have to pay $2,100—in cash—in points. The points make up for any lost profit that would result from the lower interest rate.

Bargain with the loan officer. The interest rate is negotiable, despite the opposite impression the banker may give. If you find that bank A is offering 12 percent and four points and bank B is offering 14 percent and no points, try to use the best of each against the other and negotiate a better loan than either bank is offering.

It may help to move your checking and savings account to the bank that will be giving you a loan. If your bank won't give you the lowest interest rate in town, tell your loan officer that you will be moving your accounts to another lending institution.

The best advice I can give is take some time and compare. The lending game changes its rules almost every day, but you can make the most of it by learning the new rules as they are developed.

Shopping for a lender may seem to be a formidible task, but it can actually be quite easy. One way to find a good lender is to ask the experts. Talk to a real estate broker or a real estate attorney. They will be familiar with the lenders in your area and can point you in the right direction.

You should be familiar with the restrictions you'll face from a conventional lender. Most will only lend you 75 to 80 percent of the appraised value of the property, leaving you with the remaining 20 to 25 percent to come up with yourself—or to work out with the sellers, as we've already discussed.

Another important factor in dealing with banks is that, as a general rule, they will not allow your monthly mortgage payment to be greater than 25 to 28 percent of your monthly income. Furthermore, a number of lenders will not allow your total debt payments (including the house payment, car payments, etc.) to exceed 33 percent of your monthly income. If you can live with these rules, you can usually get the loan you need—if you have good credit.

Your Credit Rating

Everyone has a credit rating today, thanks to the computer revolution. When you apply for a loan, the lender can ask for a credit report. Almost instantly your credit habits are an open book. And the story that book tells may determine whether or not you qualify for the loan.

Getting credit for the first time is a problem for young adults just getting started and for many newly divorced people, especially women who depended on their husbands' credit. It can be a frustrating "Catch-22"; you can't get a credit card because you don't have credit, and you can't get credit because you don't have a credit card. The answer is to start out slowly and build a good credit history.

Anyone with money can open a checking account, so that's the place to start. If you can put aside a small amount each month, open a savings account as well. You should never bounce a check, of course, but it is especially vital when you're starting out that you keep a clean record by never writing a check against insufficient funds.

The second step is getting your first credit card. Many major department stores offer free digital watches or other trinkets if you will apply for a credit card. If you have a steady job and have been maintaining your checking and savings accounts, you will likely be granted a small line of credit at Sears or J. C. Penney. Purchase a relatively inexpensive item—under $50—and pay it off promptly. Do not ever pay late; it will kill your credit before it gets a chance to breathe.

The third step will almost take care of itself. Once you have had a card—any card—for a few months and have shown yourself to be a good risk, you will be able to pick up other department store cards right and left. In fact, one day you'll come home and find that some store you've never even heard of has granted you a $500 line of credit.

It gets a little heady here if you haven't had experience with these plastic wonders. They are actually two-edged weapons, and if you fall into the all-American credit card trap you'll be in trouble for years. Use them carefully and never trust them.

A Mastercard or Visa will be the next step, maybe less than a year after you open your first checking account. Now you're in the big times, with a total credit line in the low thousands. Then a check-guarantee Visa through your bank with overdraft protection. If you ever overdrew a check, it will be covered by your line of credit. Congratulations; you've climbed on the carousel of credit. Stay in control of your debt and you'll find it can be a powerful tool. Lose control and it will be a nightmare.

Finding out your own credit rating is easy. Get out your phone book and look in the Yellow Pages under "Credit Bureaus" or "Credit Reporting Agencies." One phone call and a few dollars is all it takes to find out your credit rating. Tell the person who answers that you want a credit report for yourself, and let that person take it from there.

When you get your credit report, look for problems that might stand in the way of getting a loan. You may be surprised to find out that you bought two live moray eels at Walt's Sea Shop in California and never paid for them. Credit ratings have been demolished by uncaring computers too many times, and you may be an unknowing victim. Write a letter to Walt, asking for proof of your purchase. Chances are that it is a simple case of mistaken identity that can be cleared up quickly.

A clean credit record is essential for getting that needed financing, and researching your record is as easy as dialing the telephone.

Working with bankers isn't hard, once you understand what makes them tick: guaranteed return on investment. They aren't paid to take chances on some wild-eyed investor with a poor credit history. Nor are they paid to make loans that aren't fully secured by plenty of equity. Bankers love security. Understand that, and you won't have trouble working with them.

Paying Early

When you get a loan, whether it's from the sellers or from a bank, ask about paying the loan early. If your mortgage is from a private individual—the seller—you very likely can ask for a discount. If the mortgage is given by a mortgage lender—a savings and loan, perhaps—then you will likely be charged a prepayment penalty.

The reason for this difference is that a bank is in the business of making money through interest income, and has little desire to have you pay the loan back early. Bankers know how much income they are losing when you prepay. Sellers, on the other hand, may get tired of small monthly payments. A year or so after the sale—especially around December—they may be so happy to get a large chunk of cash that they'll even discount the remaining principal.

I've turned this tendency into a real advantage. Let's presume I have a $10,000 mortgage that I owe to the previous owners. Every time I send a payment I attach a note, letting them know that I will be happy to pay the balance of the mortgage early if they will discount it. If the sellers are interested, I ask for at least a 25 to 30 percent discount. In the example, I will pay off the mortgage in a lump sum *if* they are willing to accept $7,000 for it. If they won't agree to the discount, no problem—I can continue making my monthly payments.

QPL—The Quick-Payment Loan

What I'm about to propose is nearly unAmerican. If you can afford the higher payments, why not consider a short-term loan, rather than a full thirty-year loan? I know that conventional wisdom has it that the longer you have to pay the better off you are, but consider the savings, comparing a ten-, fifteen-, and thirty-year repayment schedule on the same debt. We'll use $70,000 at 12 percent interest in each example:

A. $70,000 @ 12% for ten years.

Payments:	$1,004.30 × 120 = $120,515.18
Principal:	$ 70,000.00
Interest paid:	$ 50,515.18

B. $70,000 @ 12% for fifteen years.

Payments:	$ 840.12 × 180 = $151,220.44
Principal:	$ 70,000.00
Interest paid:	$ 81,220.44

C. $70,000 @ 12% for thirty years.

Payments:	$ 720.03 × 360 = $259,206.66
Principal:	$ 70,000.00
Interest paid:	$189,206.66

Let's compare: If you took out a thirty-year loan and managed to pay it off in fifteen years, you would save $107,986.22 (189,206.22 − 81,220.44); if you could pay it off in ten years, your savings would be $138,691.48 (189.206.66 − 50,515.18). Quite a savings!

If you can't afford the higher payments at first, you may want to take out the thirty-year loan to begin with and stick with the lower payments until you can afford to pay more. But if the opportunity arises—say rents go up, or you pay off the seller's equity, raising your positive cash flow—it's a great idea to pay early.

For example, let's say you pay the $720.03 payments on a thirty-year loan for the first four years. After four years, however, you can afford to pay an additional $400 per month. How much will you save in interest payments? And when will the loan be paid off?

If that seems to be a tough question, you should learn to use a financial calculator. But even if you can't yet figure out such a problem, there are people who can. We're back to using experts. You don't even really have to know how to calculate loan payments. Open the Yellow Pages again, this time looking under "Amortization Services" or "Calculation Services." For a minimal charge—maybe five to ten dollars—they will calculate loan payments for you.

Back to the example: At the end of four years (48 payments), the loan balance will be $68,773.73. If you continue to pay $720.03, you'll have 312 payments left; by paying $1,120.03, you'll only have to make 96 more payments to pay off the loan. Savings:

Interest on 312 payments @ $720.03	$155,871.49
Interest on 96 payments @ $1,120.03	$ 38,387.43
Savings	$117,484.06

By the way, when you pay the extra $400 per month, you'll not only save over $100,000 in interest, you'll also finish paying off the loan in only eight more years—cutting a thirty-year loan down to twelve years! Wouldn't it be nice to have the loan paid off before the kids went to college . . . or in time for a nice retirement . . . or . . .

And best of all, once the loan is paid off, your positive cash flow from rental income skyrockets. No more monthly mortgage payments.

As another example of QPL, let's assume that at the end of the first four years you *can't* make an additional $400 monthly payment, but your Aunt Sally dies suddenly, leaving you $10,000. What would happen if you gave the lender that money?

Let's go back to the original terms:

$70,000 @ 12% for thirty years

Payment $720.03	
Balance at the end of four years:	$ 68,773.73
Cash payment:	$ 10,000.00
Balance due:	$ 58,773.73

Continuing to pay the $720.03, you'll have only 171 payments left, instead of 312. How much interest will you save?

Interest on 312 payments @ $702.03: $155,871.49
Interest on 171 payments @ $702.03: $ 63,828.91

Savings $ 92,042.58

Aunt Sally did you a better favor than she knew! By applying that money to your debt, you can save over $92,000 in interest payments *and* pay the loan off 11.75 years early. *Now* are you convinced that QPL may be the way to go? The temptation will be to spend the $10,000 windfall—or the extra $400-a-month income—on cruises, cars, and cast-iron cats from Cuba; especially in the case of Aunt Sally's $10,000, which is "free money." But before you book that cruise, call your friendly amortization service first and find out exactly how much you could save in interest payments by paying early.

I know the idea is radical, but the savings are incredible. The difference in how quickly the principal is paid off may make the extra burden worthwhile. I realize that a quick payoff may not be profitable in every situation. But if you can afford the extra expense (see "feeding the alligators" in this chapter), your equity build-up and interest savings may help you achieve your goals all that much faster.

If you talk to conventional lenders, at least ask them for a ten- and fifteen-year repayment schedule. If a shorter term loan doesn't cause an alligator to hatch, consider giving up a little extra profit now in exchange for an enormous savings in interest payments. The QPL method will become more important under the new tax law since interest is not as valuable a deduction as it was under the old law.

Private Investors

Finding private investors with enough money to pay cash for property isn't going to be easy; in fact, few investors even try. Nevertheless, when interest rates are prohibitive and few buyers are willing or able to get a new loan, some sellers—the ones who have considerable equity in their properties—will be willing to discount their selling price for an all-cash deal. If you can find such sellers—not a hard task when interest rates are soaring—ask how much they would accept. They may be willing to discount their selling prices by as much as 50 percent.

As in the earlier example, prepare a detailed outline for your prospective partner. Be ready to back up your claims with facts and figures, and you may have a great deal. Well-heeled investors who can afford cash purchases may not have the time to uncover such bargains, and they will pay well for your bird-dogging.

Government Loans

Uncle Sam always has money to lend, and it seems a new loan program is available every week. There are state loans and federal loans, and occasionally your city or county may have special rehab loans available. Most mortgage lenders can fill you in on the latest government programs, or you can contact the local, state, or federal housing authorities for current information.

Feeding the Alligators

I warned you against getting involved with negative cash flow (remember Stephen Wayner's golden rule: "Thou shalt have a positive cash flow.") However, there are a few techniques for turning negatives into positives that I'd like to share with you. If the deal is right, consider these options:

1. Equity Sharing
One good way to turn negative rental cash flow into positive is *equity sharing*. There are a few pitfalls that I will point out, and it isn't the best solution in every case; but it can turn an alligator into a money-maker.

Equity sharing means, not surprisingly, that you are going to share your equity in a property. You will be sharing it with your tenant, and, in exchange, your tenant will pay a higher rent to cover the negative cash flow. Maybe this concept will be best illustrated by example:

I own one house on which the total payment is $802 per month. The average rental rate on such a house is $550, leaving me with $252 to pay out of my own pocket. Rather than feed my alligator, however, I made the following proposal to my tenants: If they would pay the entire $802 per month for three years, I would give them one-half ownership in the house. At the end of three years, we would sell the house and split any profit over and above what I originally paid for it.

The benefits to my tenants are obvious: They are finally able to take their first steps out of the land of renters and into the land of home owners. It might have been several more years before they could save up enough for a down payment, and even longer before they could qualify for a conventional loan. As long as they can make the payment, they are partners in that home, and when it is sold they will have enough money to buy a home of their own.

I have four benefits: First, I can claim a depreciation expense for the entire period, saving money on my taxes. Second, I have eliminated the negative cash flow that would have cost me $3,024 per year. Third, I will get half the profit on the sale of the property. And fourth, tenants with an ownership interest will generally take better care of the house. In fact, they will usually spend extra time and money fixing it up, because they know that anything they can do to raise its selling price means more money back in their pockets. So my management duties almost disappear entirely.

Now for the drawback: The biggest problem by far is the fact that you are forming a partnership with a person who obviously can't afford to buy a home. The extra expense will be anywhere from difficult to impossible for them to maintain, and when the choice is milk for the family or a stiff payment they are likely to give up on the house. Why not form the same partnership with a more financially secure person and leave the tenant out of it entirely? (You can, with an investor. Consider forming a partnership with another investor: The investor can pay the negative and split the profit after three years.) Nevertheless, equity sharing can be a simple and highly effective way of eliminating negative cash flow. Tenants are generally very enthusiastic about the idea of owning their own homes.

I do not have the space in this book to explain the mechanics of setting up an equity-sharing arrangement with your tenants. For further information you can contact me and I will be happy to send you details on home study courses that will answer your questions and get you started.

2. Options

There are two different instruments that are often called options, but one is more than an option. One is a purchase option, and the other is a purchase option and lease, also called a "lease option."

In simple terms, a purchase option is the right given by the owner of property (called the optionor) to another party (called the optionee), by which that party can purchase the property within a certain period of time, for a specified sum. If I promise to sell you my home for $80,000 any time within the next six months, you have an option to purchase it for that price. You may choose to exercise your option, or you may allow it to expire.

A lease option includes an option *and* a normal lease. With a lease option you will rent the property for a period of time, and a portion of each month's rent may be applied toward the down payment when you exercise the option.

The purchase option can be used in situations when the seller doesn't need to move immediately but is looking for a buyer. With a six-month purchase option, for example, you have time to find another buyer who is willing to pay more than the option price for the house. For example, say Bob Cellar is trying to sell his home for $75,000. You know the house's market value is about that, but the market is slow and there are few interested buyers. Bob is in no real hurry to sell, and he isn't very flexible on price or terms. You make the following offer: You will pay him $200 for an option on his home, agreeing to buy it for the full asking price of $75,000 within six months. If you don't exercise the option, you will lose your $200 consideration, but chances are good that you can find someone willing to pay $77,000 before the option period expires. From Bob's point of view he is getting a guaranteed sale; he is assuming that you won't want to walk away from your $200, and he isn't that anxious about selling anyway. If you don't buy it he can try to sell it again in six months. If the value of Bob's house does go up $2,000, you should be able to find a buyer who is willing to pay at least $76,500. Instead of buying the home from Bob and then selling it again, you can sell the option to the new buyer for $1,500. That's $1,300 profit on a $200 investment!

With a lease option you may be able to tie up the property even longer, perhaps a year or more. This works well with sellers who have been transferred out of the state and are trying to manage a rental property long distance, or rental property owners who are just sick of managing their properties and want to sell them.

Let's use another example. Bob's brother, Jim Cellar, owns a three-bedroom house in town. He was transferred about 700 miles away and is stuck with a house that won't sell. He has tenants living in it now, but with the cat so far away the mice have come out of the woodwork to play. The yard is a mess, the interior decorating is mostly Chef Boy-ar-dee, and the rent ($600) is always late. And when it does come it misses covering the house payment by $100 every time. Jim's chances of selling the house dwindle more and more with every passing day. . . . When along comes Superinvestor (that's you).

Hearing of Jim's plight, you make an offer. If he will give you a lease option, you will pay his asking price of $75,000 (his house is a lot like Bob's) in one year. Not only that, but you will pay $700 a month, covering his entire house payment. You agree to clean up the yard and redecorate the house, so there is only a modest fee for the option privilege of, say, $50. Jim agrees to set aside $150 each month as a credit toward your down payment. Are you with me so far?

You can either move in and live there or find a renter who is willing to pay at least $600 and be responsible for cleaning up the house. With you there to keep tabs, it shouldn't be difficult to fulfill your part of the bargain. After one year the house should be worth several thousand dollars more, due to inflation and your fix-up. If you can find a buyer willing to pay $80,000 for the house, you can sell the option. You have $1,800 credit for the extra payment you have been making each month, which will go to the seller. The $1,800 has effectively reduced the amount to be financed to $73,200, so the new buyer will owe you $6,800. If you have been renting the house for $600 and paying the remaining $100 yourself, your total investment is $1,250 (including the $50 option fee). Your profit: $5,550. And you never even owned the property! You could have used this technique without having any credit. In fact, you could have filed bankruptcy the year before and you still would have made $5,550.

It's true that not many sellers will be attracted by your idea, but a purchase option or a lease option can be a real money-maker when the market is slow and sellers are having trouble finding buyers. If this sounds like something you'd like to try, contact an attorney and ask about the specific laws that govern options in your state. And if you do use an option, record it in the county wherein the property is situated. Otherwise the seller may sell the property during the option period to someone else. By recording your option, you put the world on notice that you have an interest in the property.

I've used options several times, and a personal example should serve as another good illustration. Not long ago I found a seller who had an existing mortgage of $59,880, with payments of $909, who wanted to sell his home for $60,000. Obviously, he wasn't looking for a great profit of $120; he just wanted to be rid of the high monthly mortgage payment. But the market was slow and his price was high, so month after month he continued to make the expensive mortgage payments.

I offered to rent the house for $500 a month (the market rent for such a house was $600), with an option to purchase it for his asking price of $60,000 any time within a five-year period. His objection to my offer was that it didn't solve his problem; he was still stuck with a $409 monthly negative cash flow. What he had failed to consider, however, was the deduction that

Uncle Sam allows for depreciation on investment property. With his new tax savings, his monthly loss was reduced to $150, which was manageable for him.

I immediately found a renter who had been looking for a house to buy, but couldn't afford the down payment. I rented the house to him for $600 a month, and, after he had rented the house for eight months, sold him my $60,000 option for $66,000. He now had an option to buy a house, and the owner had a much relieved monthly burden. What did I get for my effort? I had a $100 monthly income for eight months and a $6,000 profit on the sale, for a total profit of $6,800. I call this technique the "sandwich" lease option because I never actually own the property; I merely take an option from the seller and sell it to my buyer, sandwiching myself between them and taking my profit.

Here's a table that will make the numbers easier to understand:

Monthly payment	$ 500	
Monthly rent	600	
Positive cash flow	100 × 8 months:	$ 800
Option price	$60,000	
Option sold for	66,000	
Profit on sale of option		6,000
Total profit		$6,800

The sandwich lease option will work in every case where the seller has had difficulty selling his or her property and is willing to rent it to you with an option to buy it at a future date. Remember, an option does not obligate you to buy the property; it simply secures the price if and when you choose to buy it. You can exercise the option and buy the property, you can allow the option to expire, or you can sell the option to another buyer. In any case, you have solved the seller's problem and made money for yourself.

Just how easy is it to set up a sandwich lease option? Well, all it takes is a little friendly negotiating, a legal form, and some common sense. You need no credit and no cash, and you have no personal liability at all. You could have filed bankruptcy the day before. Imagine the headlines:

EXTRA! EXTRA! Read All About It! Investor who just filed bankruptcy makes money in real estate with no money out of his pocket, no liability, and no credit!

If you make every offer with the idea of *solving the seller's problem* foremost in your mind, I believe you will consummate 70 to 80 percent of all your offers. Just don't be afraid to be *creative*. Use common sense and become a problem solver—*that's* the key to successful investing.

Chapter Seven Summary

I. Financing the purchase of real estate means borrowing money—usually lots of it. To do so requires knowledge of at least the following terminology:
   A. *Interest:* the cost of borrowing money.
   B. *Principal:* the amount borrowed, which must be paid back with interest.
   C. *Payment:* how the money is to be repaid.
   D. *Term:* the length of the repayment period.
   E. *Amortization:* "killing" the loan by making payments of interest and principal. If a loan is fully amortized over its term, the payments will be the same amount each time, until, at the end of the term, both the principal and interest will have been fully paid.

II. Every factor in a loan, including how it is to be amortized, is a matter of agreement between the buyer and seller. Today, financial calculators can figure out payment schedules in moments, making loan amortization a simple chore.

III. There are two parts to financing the purchase of real estate: the loan and the down payment. If you don't have the money for the down payment, you have five options:

A. *Borrow* the down payment by taking in a partner. If you know anyone with enough money for the down payment, you may have a potential partner.

B. *Nothing down* is a popular concept, but it's usually hard to convince sellers to accept all of their money in the future, and it may cost much more in higher monthly payments. Nevertheless, it's always an option to consider.

C. *Alternatives to cash,* such as cars or other assets that you own, may be acceptable to some sellers. Promissory notes or letters of credit may work, especially as binders during the escrow period.

D. *Sweat equity* is often a good down payment. The seller knows that even if the deal falls through and he is forced to repossess, at least you will have increased the value of the property.

E. *Quitting* is rarely the answer, but passing up a marginal deal for a better one down the road isn't a bad idea.

IV. Keeping the down payment low—even if you can afford a higher payment—is usually a good idea because you will pay less in taxes (due to higher mortgage payments); because when you sell you can charge a lower down payment to your buyer; and by using less of your own money you will be increasing your return on investment.

V. If the seller has a lower-than-market interest rate *and* if the loan is assumable, you should assume it. If the seller isn't sure whether or not the loan can be assumed, have an attorney review it for you. At the time of this writing, VA, FHA, and most pre-1978 loans may be assumed.

VI. If you must get conventional financing, check with several lenders. Ask them the questions outlined in this chapter and shop around. They will need to know how much equity you will have in the property to secure the loan and how good a credit risk you are. If you don't have credit you should work on establishing a good credit rating; if your rating is in trouble, clean it up.

VII. Conventional lenders will usually have shorter-term loan programs. If the cash flow is still positive, or if you can handle the negative, consider a quick-payment loan. You will build up equity much faster, save in interest payments, and you will own the property free and clear that much sooner. This has become more important under the new tax law, because the interest deduction isn't as important as it was under the old law.

VIII. Private investors can be another source of funds, especially in times of high interest rates. The government has several loans available, and you can find out about current loan programs simply by calling or writing to the housing authorities.

IX. If you find what appears to be a good deal but you are still left with a negative cash flow, you may try either equity sharing with your tenant—or another investor—or using an option. Either method will eliminate the negative, turning an alligator into a money-maker.

Chapter Seven Homework

1. Call lenders in your area. It's not hard. Pick up the phone and start calling banks, savings and loans, and mortgage companies. Ask for current rates and new loan programs that are available. Prepare a written comparison and be ready to shop seriously for a loan.

2. Purchase a financial calculator and learn to use it. If you purchase Hewlett-Packard's HP-12C and would like further help in using it to solve real estate problems, contact the following company for an excellent home-study course:

   Jodestar Seminars, Inc.
   P.O. Box 562047
   Miami, Florida 33256

3. You're almost ready to purchase your first real estate investment. The next time you sit down with a seller to negotiate, begin making concrete plans for the financing, using the various suggestions in this chapter. Find out how much equity they have available. Will they accept payments for all or part of that equity? Why or why not? Are the existing loans assumable (and if the owners don't know, how can you find out)?

4. Contact Realtors and lenders and find out about any government loan programs that are currently available. Contact the housing authority also; have them send you information.

Part Four

Write the Contract, Close the Deal

Chapter Eight

The Contract

Here is where I come into my own. As an attorney, I read contracts like most people read Wheaties boxes; I write them like most people write to mom. But I'm fully aware that my skill with contracts puts me in a minority. Therefore, I'm devoting this chapter to teaching you all I can about real estate contracts. By the time we're finished here, you should feel at ease in making your own offers, complete with added "success clauses," which I will give you.

Real estate contracts come in all shapes and sizes, and the day of a uniform contract is still in the distant future—if we ever see that day. So I'll give you a contract in generalities, and you can fill in the specifics with the help of your local attorney.

Earnest Money

A purchase offer for real estate will include (usually in the title) wording to the effect that it is a "Purchase Contract and Receipt for Deposit." The deposit mentioned is also called "earnest money." The term "earnest money" refers to a small deposit that is made to the seller by the buyer to demonstrate his earnest intent to actually buy the property.

There are several things to be aware of when you offer an earnest money agreement. First, don't think that you must give the seller $1,000. You can give as much or as little as you wish, as long as the seller is willing to accept it. I rarely give more than $500, and usually much less if the seller will take it. Second, *never* give cash (or a check made out to the seller). Always make the check payable to the title company, attorney, or real estate agent who will be handling the closing.

If the deposit is placed with the third party (lawyer, Realtor, escrow company, etc.), it may be a good idea to have your money deposited in a separate account requiring both the third party's signature and yours to take the money out of the account. Recently, a client of mine was involved in a situation in which the real estate broker went into the escrow account and used the funds for his own personal use. A two-party account would have avoided that problem.

If a seller who has listed his or her property with a broker tentatively accepts your offer, the broker may have you sign a *binder*. This is another gesture of good faith on your part, rather than a contract for sale. On the basis of this binder, the seller will take the property off the market and you agree to form a contract. But again, you never know if the deal will go through, so you need to ensure, in writing, that your deposit will be refunded if you cannot form a contract. In some states the binder (contract) is your contract to purchase, so be careful.

I read recently about a man who was convinced by the seller to give $12,000 earnest money. (The man obviously had the deposit confused with the down payment.) The earnest money is part of the total payment, so there would still have been no problem, except the man was subsequently unable to get a loan for the property and had to break the contract, and he lost his earnest money. He made two mistakes: First, he should only have given a token amount for his deposit. Second, he should have included a contingency clause in the contract that would allow him not to go through with the deal if he couldn't get financing.

One of my students always uses a letter of credit from his bank. A letter of credit does not mean that the dollars have been taken out of his bank account; it simply means that the bank is willing to guarantee the amount specified in the letter. The distinction is important: He can secure the deal with a letter of credit, tie up the property during the entire escrow period, and never take one dime out of the bank until the closing.

Another student always uses a promissory note. The note has no personal liability, and yet he can use it like cash—if the sellers are willing to accept it. The note is unsecured, and therefore totally worthless, but, surprisingly, he has had tremendous success using these notes. (I say surprisingly because I wouldn't accept an unsecured note if I were selling my home—would you?)

The Names

There is always a space on the contract for the buyer's name. If you're buying the property with a partner or spouse, both names will appear on the line. In any case, after the name you will—for reasons we will discuss shortly—include the words "and/or assigns."

If ownership is held by an individual, the other party (spouse or partner) has no legal interest in it. The property is held "severally," as opposed to "concurrently" (held by more than one owner). If there is more than one owner, the parties will either own it as tenants in common or as joint tenants.

Tenancy in common occurs when each owner has an undivided fractional interest in the property. If one owner dies his interest becomes part of his estate and is passed on to his heirs. If you own a piece of property concurrently with one or more business partners, you will likely do so as tenants in common. That way if you die your heirs will inherit your share of the property.

Joint tenancy means that the owners have an undivided interest in the property. If one owner dies his interest in the property is automatically transferred to the surviving owners. If you own a property with a business partner as joint tenants and then die, your heirs will have no claim over the property. Joint tenancy is usually the best way to concurrently own property with a spouse because it allows the property to completely escape probate, leaving the surviving spouse free to sell it if necessary.

You can decide how you want to hold the property before you buy it, and whoever is handling the closing will take care of it for you.

Filling in the Blanks

I recommend that you sit down at the kitchen table with the seller and discuss terms in plain English. Don't worry about the legalese; you can have someone translate your verbal agreement into legal terminology later. Concentrate on understanding each other's needs, and try to reach an agreement. Then take your ideas to your friendly real estate attorney and have him or her help you write the contract.

I also recommend that you use the contract approved by your local board of Realtors (any Realtor can get a copy for you). It will be more complete than the basic form you'll find in a stationery store. Your attorney can help you fill in the blanks, and you can add some of the following clauses that I've prepared to make writing offers less frightening.

I say less frightening because I've noticed a great reluctance on the part of new investors to make written offers. The whole process seems so "legal," as though making the offer is the first real step toward buying property. They are afraid of becoming enmeshed in a web of their own spinning, and, in many cases, their fears are later justified . . . if they have failed to include a few clauses that will let them get out of potentially bad deals without costing them their earnest money deposits.

Escape Clauses

An escape clause is usually a sentence or two that allows the person making the offer (offeror) literally to escape from the contract at any time. It would be more than a good idea to include escape clauses in every offer you make, and here are some of the most effective:

> 1. Buyer shall apply for a new mortgage in an amount of not less than $_____ at _____ % interest and for _____ amount of years having the monthly payment of principal and interest in the amount of $_____ per month. This contract is contingent upon buyer obtaining the aforesaid mortgage which must be prepayable without penalty and be freely assumable upon resale.

As previously mentioned, this clause can be used whenever you are going to get new financing for all or part of the purchase. If, for any reason, you cannot obtain the necessary financing, your offer is revoked and the contract is no longer binding. You are free to walk away without any loss or obligation—the whole purpose of an escape clause.

> 2. This offer is subject to buyer's partner's approval.

This simple sentence is an all-inclusive escape clause, as it allows you to back out of any deal for any reason whatsoever. I'm not suggesting that you invent an imaginary partner, but your partner can be anyone you choose, and if at any time before closing you decide not to buy the property, your partner can disapprove of the deal and everything is called off.

> 3. *"And/or assigns"*

This isn't a clause at all, but it should appear after your name on the contract. What it means is that you are reserving the right to assign your position in the contract to anyone, at any time. There are two reasons for doing this. The first is that you can "flip" the transaction before the closing. If, for example, your offer of $45,000 is accepted and you find a buyer before the closing who will pay $48,000 for it, you can simply assign the contract to the third person, making $3,000 without ever actually owning the property at all.

The second reason was suggested to me by a student. He said that if he decides that he doesn't want to close, he assigns the contract to a third person who may or may not be able to qualify for necessary financing. My student, having assigned the contract, is not in breach of contract because he had a right to assign. And the assignee is left with the other escape clause that states the offer is contingent on the buyer obtaining financing.

I personally feel that there is a legitimate reason for using "and/or assigns." Using the phrase as an escape clause, knowing that you will be assigning the contract to a third party who will not qualify for financing, is unnecessary. There are other escape clauses that are more straightforward and therefore more fair to the seller. However, if the seller will not allow any other escape clauses, always insist on "and/or assigns" in every offer—just in case.

By leaving yourself plenty of room for escape, your offers are always left open—at least to you. That should remove any fear on your part, and you can feel comfortable making as many offers as you want, knowing you can always back out without losing anything.

Don't Leave Anything to Chance

While you shouldn't be afraid of a contract, neither should you take its importance lightly. This is the tie that binds buyer and seller, and one misplaced decimal point can mean disaster. To help you check your contract-reading and direction-following skills, I've designed your third and final "fun quiz." Read all of the directions carefully before you begin, and follow every direction to the letter.

Can You Follow Directions?

For each of the ten directions below, do exactly as you are told if and only if the question below it contains fewer than three commas. However, if the direction below contains three or more commas, you should disregard both the original direction and the one below. If a direction contains a semicolon, disregard it unless it also contains a proper noun (such as the Empire State Building). On all directions use a soft pencil. (You'll want to erase your marks when you're finished, right?) If a direction ends with a question mark, answer it correctly but skip the next one. Read all ten directions before you begin.

1. In the directions given above, circle every capital letter and write them in the spaces below:

   _

2. From the letters in the answer to direction one, take away the letters in the word that means "to tell a lie." Write the remaining letters—in reverse order—in the spaces below:

   _

3. To the list of letters above, add—at the end of the list—the first three letters of the third word in direction one.

   _

4. Not everyone is right handed; if you are left handed, reverse the order of the letters in answer three:

   _

5. Disregard direction three entirely; instead, add the first three letters in the name of the capital of California:

   _

6. If pigs have wings, horns, or feathers, substitute the first three letters with the letters P-I-G:

‗ ‗

7. Have you followed every direction to the letter so far?

‗ ‗ ‗ ‗ ‗ yes   ‗ ‗ ‗ ‗ ‗ no

8. If the answer to the question above is yes, switch the third and fourth letters:

‗ ‗

9. Exchange every letter (in what you believe to be the proper list of letters at this point) with the letter that precedes it in the alphabet.

‗ ‗

10. Now that you have read every direction before doing anything (as you were instructed to do before beginning the quiz), disregard all of the first nine directions. Instead, write the last name of the author in the spaces below.

‗ ‗

Well, how did you fare? Very few will pass such a test, and yet a contract is not dissimilar. Read *all* of the contract carefully before beginning, and if you need help, don't be afraid to seek it from your local experts.

I ask in my seminars how many people have been bitten by a lion. So far I've never had a hand go up. Then I ask how many have been bitten by a horse; I get a few responses. Then how many have been bitten by a dog. That raises quite a few hands. Last I ask how many have been bitten by a mosquito. Of course, every hand in the room goes up. The point: It's always the little things that get you.

Writing a contract is like going on vacation: Even though you're sure you've thought of everything, something is usually left behind. I've had a nasty run-in with such a situation personally.

I bought a house recently for $59,000. It was small, but the owners had spared no expense in fixing it up. They had installed a special "popcorn" ceiling, a brand new 22.2 cubic foot Westinghouse refrigerator, a new Amana stove, three air conditioning units, a brand new washer and dryer combination, Levelor blinds, etc.

Being a real estate attorney, and knowing almost every-thing there is to know about real estate contracts, I wrote a brief description of the appliances, which were to be included in the purchase. I inspected the premises shortly before the closing day, and everything was in working order. Imagine my unpleas-ant surprise when, a week later, I looked in on my latest in-vestment and was greeted not by a gorgeous 22.2 cubic foot Westinghouse refrigerator, but by a worn-out, ten-year-old 7.9 cubic foot off-brand junker.

What was my mistake? I had written ''refrigerator'' on the contract. Don't make the same mistake. Write down a com-plete description, and even include the serial number of each appliance that is to be included in the sale. The extra informa-tion can't hurt, and it can avoid unpleasant surprises later.

Right of First Refusal

If the seller is willing to finance part of the sale for you, insist that you have the ''right of first refusal.'' The actual phrase that you must include in the contract is:

> Buyer shall have the
> right of first refusal
> to buy the mortgage.

Stripping down the legalese into English, this is the right that you have to purchase the mortgage before anyone else. If, for example, $6,000 is left owing on the mortgage and the seller has an offer of $4,000, you can buy the mortgage for the same price. It cannot be sold to anyone without your knowledge, and you may—if you wish—buy it at the same price that anyone else offers (and the seller accepts).

I was involved in just such a situation. I bought a house and the seller gave me a $10,000 mortgage. I made my monthly payments on time, and I had, of course, insisted on the right of

DEPOSIT RECEIPT AND CONTRACT FOR SALE AND PURCHASE

residing at _____ , his wife,

the seller, and   hereinafter called

residing at _____ , his wife,

hereinafter called

the buyer, hereby agree that the seller shall sell and the buyer shall buy the following described property UPON THE TERMS AND CONDITIONS HEREINAFTER SET FORTH, which shall include the STANDARD FOR REAL ESTATE TRANSACTIONS set forth on reverse side of this contract.

1. LEGAL DESCRIPTION of real estate located in _____ County, Florida:

Personal property included:

Street address:

Seller represents that the property can be used for the following purposes:

2. Purchase price and Method of Payment; Purchase price is _____ Dollars.

Deposit to be held in trust by _____ $ _____

Approximate principal balance of first mortgage to which conveyance shall

be subject, if any. Mortgage holder _____ $ _____

Interest _____ % per annum; Method of payment _____ $ _____

Other:

Cash, certified or local cashier's check on closing and delivery of deed (or

such greater or lesser amount as may be necessary to complete payment of

purchase price after credits, adjustments and prorations). $ _____

3. TIME FOR ACCEPTANCE: If this contract is not executed by the seller and buyer on or before _____ the aforesaid deposit shall be, at the option of the buyer, returned to him and this agreement shall be null and void. The date of contract, for purposes of performance, shall be regarded as the date when the last one of the seller and buyer has signed this contract.

4. CLOSING DATE: This contract shall be closed and the deed and possession shall be delivered on or about _____ days after this contract has been executed by both the buyer and the seller.

5. EVIDENCE OF TITLE: (Check ☐ (1) or ☐ (2)) Within _____ days from the date of this contract, the seller shall, at his expense, deliver to the buyer or his attorney in accordance with Standard A on reverse side either: (1) abstract (2) Title guarantee.

6. FINANCING: If the purchase price or any part thereof is to be financed by a third party loan, this Contract for Sale and Purchase, hereinafter referred to as "Contract", is conditioned upon the Buyer obtaining a firm commitment for said loan within 60 days

from date hereof, at an interest rate not to exceed _____ %; term of _____ years,
and in the principal amount of $ _____ . Buyer agrees to make application for,
and to use reasonable diligence to obtain said loan. Should Buyer fail to obtain same, or to waive Buyer's rights hereunder within said
time, either party may cancel Contract.

7. RESTRICTIONS AND EASEMENTS: The buyer shall take title subject to: (a) Zoning and/or restrictions and prohibitions imposed by governmental authority, (b) Restrictions and matters appearing on the plat and/or common to the subdivision, (c) Public utility easements of record, provided said easements are located on the side or rear lines of the property and are not more than six feet
in width, (d) Other

Further provided that none of the foregoing interferes with the use of the property for the purposes as stated in this contract.

8. TYPEWRITTEN OR HANDWRITTEN PROVISIONS: Typewritten or handwritten provisions inserted in this form shall control
all printed provisions in conflict therewith.

9. SPECIAL CLAUSES:

WITNESSES: (Two are required)

Executed by Buyer on _____

_____ (SEAL)
_____ (SEAL)

_____   _____
                                   Buyer

COMMISSION TO BROKER: The seller hereby recognizes _____
as the broker in this transaction, and agrees to pay as commission _____ % of the gross sales price, the sum of

Dollars($ _____) or one-half of the deposit in case same is forfeited by the buyer through failure to perform, as
compensation for service rendered, provided same does not exceed the full amount of the commission.

Executed by Seller on _____

WITNESSES: (Two are required)

_____ (SEAL)
_____ (SEAL)

_____   _____
                                   Seller

Deposit received on _____ to be held subject to this contract; if check, subject to clearance.

By _____

_____   _____   (   )
   Broker   Attorney

Form 2050

A. EVIDENCE OF TITLE: 1. An abstract of title prepared or brought current by a reputable and existing abstract firm (if not existing then certified as correct by an existing firm) purporting to be an accurate synopsis of the instruments affecting the title to subject real property recorded in the public records of the county wherein the land is situated, through date of Contract. An abstract shall commence with the earliest public records, or such later date as may be customary in the county wherein the land is situated. Seller shall convey a marketable title in accordance with Title Standards adopted from time to time by The Florida Bar, subject only to liens, encumbrances, exceptions or qualifications set forth in this Contract and those which shall be discharged by Seller at or before closing. Upon closing of this transaction such abstract shall become the property of Buyer, subject to the right of retention thereof by first mortgagee until fully paid; or 2. a title insurance commitment issued by a qualified title insuror agreeing to issue to Buyer, upon recording of the deed to Buyer, an Owner's policy of title insurance in the amount of the purchase price, insuring title of the Buyer to the real property, subject only to liens, encumbrances, exceptions or qualifications set forth in the Contract and those which shall be discharged by Seller at or before closing. Buyer shall have 45 days, if abstract, or 15 days, if title commitment, from date of receiving evidence of title to examine same. If title is found defective, Buyer shall, within 15 days thereafter, notify Seller in writing specifying defect(s). If said defect(s) render title unmarketable, Seller shall have 180 days from receipt of notice within which to remove said defect(s), and if Seller is unsuccessful in removing them within said time, Buyer shall have the option of either (1) accepting the title as it then is, or (2) demanding a refund of all monies paid hereunder which shall forthwith be returned to Buyer and thereupon Buyer and Seller shall be released as to one another, of all further obligations under the Contract; however, Seller agrees that he will, if title is found to be unmarketable, use diligent effort to correct the defect(s) in title within the time provided therefor, including the bringing of necessary suits.

B. EXISTING MORTGAGES: Seller shall furnish a statement from the mortgagee setting forth principal balance, method of payment, interest rate and whether the mortgage is in good standing. If a mortgage requires approval of the Buyer by the mortgage in order to avoid default, or for assumption by the Buyer of said mortgage, and (a) the mortgagee does not approve the Buyer, the Buyer may rescind the Contract, or (2) require an increase in the interest rate or charge a fee for any reason in excess of $250.00, the Buyer may rescind the Contract unless Seller elects to pay such increase or excess. Seller shall pay 50% of such fee up to $125.00. Buyer will apply for mortgage approval. The amount of any escrow deposits held by mortgagee shall be credited to Seller.

C. PURCHASE MONEY MORTGAGES: The purchase money note and mortgage, if any, shall provide for a 15 day grace period in the event of default; shall provide for right of prepayment in whole or in part without penalty; shall not provide for acceleration in event of resale of the property. Said mortgage shall require the owner of the property encumbered to keep all prior liens and encumbrances in good standing and forbid the owner of the property from accepting modifications of or future advances under prior mortgage(s).

D. SURVEY: The Buyer, within time allowed for delivery of evidence of title and examination thereof, may have the property surveyed at his expense. If the survey, certified by a registered Florida surveyor, shows any encroachment on said property or that improvements intended to be located on the subject property in fact encroach on lands of others, or violate any of the Contract convenants, the same shall be treated as a title defect. Any survey prepared in connection with this transaction may include a description of the property under the Florida Coordinate System as defined in Chapter 177, Florida Statutes.

E. TERMITES AND ROOF: The Buyer, within time allowed for delivery of evidence of title and examination thereof, or no later than 10 days prior to closing, whichever date occurs last, may have the improvements inspected at Buyer's expense by a Certified Pest Control Operator and/or Roofer to determine whether there is any visible active termite infestation or visible existing damages from termite infestation in the improvements or dry rot or any roof repairs deemed needed. If Buyer is informed of either or both of the foregoing, then Seller shall pay valid costs of treatment and repair of all damages up to 3% of Purchase Price. Should such costs exceed that amount, Buyer shall have the option of cancelling Contract within 15 days after receipt of contractor's repair estimate to 3% of said Purchase Price. "Termite" shall be deemed to include all wood destroying insects.

F. INGRESS AND EGRESS: Seller covenants and warrants that there is ingress and egress to the property.

G. LEASES: Seller shall, not less than 15 days prior to closing, furnish to Buyer copies of all written leases and estoppel letters from each tenant specifying the nature and duration of said tenant's occupancy, rental rates and advanced rent and security deposits paid by tenant. In the event Seller is unable to obtain such letters from each tenant, the same information shall be furnished by Seller to Buyer within said time period in the form of a Seller's affidavit, and Buyer may thereafter contact tenants to confirm such information. Seller shall deliver and assign all original leases to Buyer at closing.

H. LIENS: Seller shall, both as to the realty and personalty being sold hereunder, furnish to Buyer at time of closing an affidavit attesting to the absence unless otherwise provided for herein of any financing statements, claims of lien or portential lienors known to Seller and further attesting that there have been no improvements to the property for 90 days immediately preceding date of closing. If the property has been improved within said time, Seller shall deliver releases or waivers of all mechanics liens, executed by general contractors, subcontractors, suppliers and materialmen, and further reciting that in fact all bills for work to the subject property which could serve as a basis for a mechanic's lien have been paid or will be paid at closing.

I. PLACE OF CLOSING: Closing shall be held at the office of the attorney or other closing agent designated by Buyer.

J. TIME: Any reference herein to time periods of less than 6 days, in the computation thereof exclude Saturdays, Sundays and legal holidays, and any time period provided for herein which shall end on a Saturday, Sunday or legal holiday shall extend to 5:00 p.m. of the next full business day.

K. DOCUMENTS FOR CLOSING: Seller shall furnish deed, mechanic's lien affidavit, assignments of leases, and any corrective instruments that may be required in connection with perfecting the title. Buyer shall furnish closing statement, mortgage, mortgage note, and financing statements.

L. EXPENSES: Documentary stamps which are required to be affixed to the instrument of conveyance, cost of recording any corrective instruments and recording of purchase money mortgage to Seller, and cost of recording any corrective instruments shall be paid by Seller. Documentary stamps to be affixed to the note or note secured by the purchase money mortgage, cost of recording the deed, financing statements and intangible tax shall be paid by Buyer.

M. PRORATION OF TAXES (REAL AND PERSONAL): Taxes shall be prorated based on the current year's tax with due allowance made for maximum allowable discount and homestead or other exemptions if allowed for said year. Any tax proration based on an estimate may at request of either party to the transaction, be subsequently readjusted upon receipt of tax bill on condition that a statement to that effect is set forth in the closing statement.

N. SPECIAL ASSESSMENT LIENS: Certified, confirmed and ratified special assessment liens as of closing (and not as of date of Contract) are to be paid by Seller. Pending liens as of date of closing shall be assumed by Buyer, provided, however, that where the improvement has been substantially completed as of the date of closing such pending lien shall be considered as certified, confirmed or ratified and Seller shall, at closing, be charged an amount equal to the last estimate by the public body of the assessment for the improvement.

O. PROPERTY INSPECTION, REPAIR: Seller warrants that all major appliances, heating, cooling, electrical, plumbing systems, and machinery and sea wall if any are in working condition and good repair as of closing. Buyer may, at his expense, have inspections made of said items by licensed persons dealing in the repair and maintenance thereof, and shall report in writing to Seller such items as found not in working condition prior to taking possession thereof. Valid reported failures and repairs shall be corrected at Seller's cost with funds therefor escrowed at closing or repaired prior to closing at the buyers option. Seller agrees to provide access for inspection.

P. RISK OF LOSS: If the improvements are damaged by fire or other casualty prior to closing, and costs of restoring same does not exceed 5% of the Assessed Valuation of the improvements so damaged, cost of restoration shall be an obligation of the Seller and closing shall proceed pursuant to the terms of Contract with cost therefor escrowed at closing or repaired prior to closing at the buyers option. In the event the cost of repair or restoration exceeds 5% of the assessed valuation of the improvements so damaged, Buyer shall have the option of either taking the property as is, together with either the said 5% or any insurance proceeds payable by virtue of such loss or damage, or of canceling Contract and receiving return of deposit(s) made hereunder.

Q. MAINTENANCE: Notwithstanding provisions of Standard O, between Contract date and closing date, personal property referred to in Standard O and real property, including lawn, shrubbery and pool, if any, shall be maintained by Seller in conditions they existed as of Contract date, ordinary wear and tear excepted.

R. ASSIGNABILITY: This Contract is freely assignable at any time prior to closing.

S. PROCEEDS OF SALE AND CLOSING PROCEDURE: The deed shall be recorded upon clearance of funds and evidence of title continued at Buyer's expense, to show title in Buyer, without any encumbrances or change which would render Seller's title unmarketable, from the date of the last evidence and the cash proceeds of sale shall be held in escrow by Seller's attorney or by such other escrow agent as may be mutually agreed upon for a period of not longer than 5 days from and after closing date. If Seller's title is rendered unmarketable, Buyer shall within said 5 day period, notify Seller in writing of the defect and Seller shall have 30 days from date of receipt of such notification to cure said defect. In the event Seller fails to timely cure said defect, all monies paid hereunder shall, upon written demand therefor and within 10 days thereafter, be returned to Buyer and simultaneously with such repayment, Buyer shall vacate the premises and reconvey the property in question to the Seller by special warranty deed. In the event a portion of the purchase price is to be derived from institutional financing or re-financing, the requirements of the lending institution as to place, time and procedures for closing and for disbursement of mortgage proceeds, shall control, anything in this Contract to the contrary notwithstanding. Provided, however, that the Seller shall have the right to require from such lending institution at closing a commitment that it will not withhold disbursement of mortgage proceeds as a result of any title defect attributable to Buyer-mortgagor.

T. ESCROW: Any escrow agent receiving funds is authorized and agrees by acceptance thereof to promptly deposit and to hold same in escrow and to disburse same subject to clearance thereof in accordance with terms and conditions of Contract. Failure of clearance of funds shall not excuse performance by the buyer. In the event of doubt as to his duties or liabilities under the provisions of this Contract, the escrow agent may in his sole discretion, continue to hold the monies which are the subject of this escrow until the parties mutually agree to the disbursement thereof, or until a judgment of a court of competent jurisdiction shall determine the rights of the parties thereto, or he may deposit all the monies then held pursuant to this Contract with the Clerk of the Circuit Court of the County having jurisdiction of the dispute, and upon notifying all parties concerned of such action, all liability on the part of the escrow agent shall fully terminate, except to the extent of accounting for any monies theretofore delivered out of escrow. If a licensed real estate broker, the escrowee will comply with provisions of Section 475.25(1)(c), F.S., as amended. In the event of any suit between Buyer and Seller wherein the escrow agent is made a party by virtue of acting as such escrow agent hereunder, or in the event of any suit wherein escrow agent interpleads the subject matter of this escrow, the escrow agent shall be entitled to recover a reasonable attorney's fee and costs incurred, said fees and costs to be charged and assessed as court costs in favor of the prevailing party. Escrow agent shall immediately deliver the escrowed deposit to buyer in the event the conditions set forth in Standard W occur and no release from either party shall be necessary. All parties agree that the escrow agent shall not be liable to any party or person whomsoever for misdelivery to Buyer or Seller of monies subject to this escrow, unless such misdelivery shall be due to wilful breach of this Contract or gross negligence on the part of the escrow agent.

U. ATTORNEY FEES AND COSTS: In connection with any litigation including appellate proceedings arising out of this Contract, the prevailing party shall be entitled to recover reasonable attorney's fees and costs.

V. DEFAULT: If Buyer fails to perform this Contract within the time specified, the deposit(s) paid by the Buyer aforesaid may be retained by or for the account ¼ to Seller and ¼ to Broker as liquidated damages, consideration for the execution of this Contract and in full settlement of any claims; whereupon all parties shall be relieved of all obligations under the Contract. If, for any reason other than failure of Seller to render his title marketable after diligent effort, Seller fails, neglects or refuses to perform this Contract, the Buyer may seek specific performance or elect to receive the return of his deposit(s) without thereby waiving any action for damages resulting from Seller's breach, and sue Seller for any damages allowed by law.

W. NOTICE: The Seller agrees upon receiving 24 hours notice to allow the Buyer or his agent to inspect the subject property several times prior to closing.

X. PRORATIONS AND INSURANCE: Taxes, assessments, rent, interest, insurance and other expenses and revenue of said property shall be prorated as of date of closing. Buyer shall have the option of taking over any existing policies of insurance on the property, if assumable, in which event premiums shall be prorated. The cash at closing shall be increased or decreased as may be required by said prorations. All references in Contract to prorations as of date of closing will be deemed "date of occupancy" if occupancy occurs prior to closing, unless otherwise provided for herein.

Y. CONVEYANCE: Seller shall convey title to the aforesaid real property by statutory warranty deed subject only to matters contained in Paragraph VII hereof. Personal property shall, at the request of Buyer, be conveyed by an absolute bill of sale with warranty of title, subject to such liens as may be otherwise provided for herein.

Z. OTHER AGREEMENTS: No prior or present agreements or representations shall be binding upon any of the parties hereto unless incorporated in this Contract. No modification or change in this contract shall be valid or binding upon the parties unless in writing, executed by the parties to be bound thereby.

first refusal. The seller suddenly needed cash, and he had an asset: the mortgage. He found a buyer who was willing to pay $6,000 for the loan (there was $9,850 owing on it). Having the right of first refusal, I was able to purchase the mortgage for the same price, paying $6,000 and saving $3,850—plus interest. The sellers shouldn't mind having the clause in the contract; they'll get their full $6,000, whether it comes from you or another party.

The right of first refusal is such an obviously useful clause that you *must* include it every time a seller is willing to give you financing. If you are unsure about its legality or where or how it should be placed in a contract, have your attorney assist you. If you live in a state where closings are handled by a title company, your title officer can probably help you. But keep in mind that title officers are not qualified to render legal opinions or to ensure legalities. When in doubt, use an expert.

Sample Contract

On pages 216–219 is an actual contract (used in Florida). Keep in mind that the contract you will be using may or may not look exactly like this one. Again, I strongly recommend that you have professional help every time you make a written offer.

Once you've filled out the contract, you're ready to present it to the seller. The seller can either accept it, reject it, or make a counter offer. In any case, you're on your way to buying your first investment property. And all you've had to do was use the education found in this book and a little common sense.

Chapter Eight Summary

1. The written purchase offer consists of two parts: the offer to purchase real estate and an earnest money agreement. The earnest money is a show of

good faith as well as a legal binder, but it need not be a large sum of money. Give the smallest amount the seller will accept, in the form of a check, money order, or promissory note made payable to the title company, agent, or attorney who will be handling the closing.

2. The names of the buyers should be followed by the words "and/or assigns." If there is more than one buyer, you should specify whether you will be buying as joint tenants or tenants in common.

3. The contract should be filled out carefully and completely. Any expert can help you with your offer, but I recommend using a real estate attorney, the only one qualified to render a legal opinion as to the validity of the offer.

4. An escape clause is a clause inserted into the offer that will allow the buyer to "escape" from the contract any time before closing. You should use at least one escape clause in every offer.

5. If you can think of any detail not covered by the contract, add a clause to cover it! Have your attorney put the clause in legalese to make sure it is legally binding.

6. If a buyer is giving you owner financing, insist in your offer on the right of first refusal. If he or she ever sells your contract, you have first dibs on it.

Chapter Eight Homework

1. Get a purchase offer form from a Realtor. Fill it out as though you were going to present a bona fide offer. What problems did you encounter? What blanks did you find hard to fill? Have a friendly Realtor or other expert who deals with offers every day give you a hand.

2. Now that you've had practice, make an actual written offer. Yes, you read that right: Make a written offer. You should by now have implemented what you've learned in this book, and you should have found at least one possible deal. When you make your offer, offer less than you actually want to pay. If the sellers accept, you're on your way to your first real estate deal, but you're still protected by your escape clauses; if they reject your offer, you've lost nothing; and if they make a counter offer, you're still in the driver's seat.

Chapter
Nine

Escrow and
Closing

The Escrow Period

The escrow period is the time between acceptance of the offer and settlement (the final day of closing). It can be as short as one day and as long as you want to make it. You want enough time to have the property professionally inspected, to get the title searched, to get any necessary financing, and, if you want to sell quickly, to find a buyer if possible. The sellers need enough time to pack up and move, and probably to make arrangements for the closing of their new home. Whoever is going to give you financing will need time to approve your credit, and your attorney or escrow agent will need time to prepare all of the necessary legal paper work.

If you ask for an extended closing, such as six months, the seller will probably balk and ask for a much shorter escrow period. Therefore it is necessary that it be long enough for everything to get done without being so long that it is inconvenient.

Each situation will dictate the length of the escrow period. To give you an idea of both extremes, I'll use examples modeled from actual cases. In the first one, Gus, an investor, found a home that was for sale by owner. The owner was three months behind on his payments and absolutely could not pay one more cent on the house. What equity he had in the property he was willing to give up if Gus would make up the delinquent payments and assume the loan. Gus wrote an offer agreeing to do so, and the contract was signed. Since he was agreeing to begin making payments immediately, there was no advantage to Gus in having a long escrow period. Instead he pushed the paper work through quickly, closing the deal within two weeks. A three-month escrow period would have meant that Gus would be stuck with even more delinquent payments on a property for which he would have neither title nor possession.

In the second example we'll use Gus again. This time he has found a home for which Gloria, the owner, is asking $75,000. Gloria isn't in an extreme hurry to sell, and she has turned down several offers below $73,000. Gus offers her the full $75,000 *if* she'll accept a six-month escrow period. Now he is getting six months to line up a buyer and she is getting her full asking price. This extended escrow technique is very similar in many respects to a six-month purchase option, but it gives the seller the feeling that the buyer is locked more securely into the deal.

Between those two extremes the escrow period is completely up to the buyer and seller. Talk about it while you are in your preliminary negotiations and you won't have any problem.

Inspection of Documents

It's a good idea to have your attorney take a look at all of the seller's documents some time prior to closing (during the escrow period). In fact, you can make the offer contingent upon your attorney's approval.

In Florida we use a mortgage and note, rather than a deed of trust, to finance real estate. The mortgages can be quite confusing and almost unreadable to someone not familiar with the legal jargon. Therefore, when I'm the purchaser I suggest including the following clause in every purchase offer:'

All closing documents must be reviewed by Purchaser's attorney and approved by same prior to closing.

In fact, this is a good escape clause. If my attorney does not approve the documentation, then I don't have to close. My deposit should be returned to me. Of course, if I'm the seller, I'd want the clause to read: "Seller's attorney approval. . . ."

The Escrow Account

Most payments you make on your mortgage or deed of trust will include your interest on the loan and a portion of the principal. In addition, most lenders will collect 1/12 of your annual taxes and insurance charges, which they keep in an escrow—or impound—account. It's easy to see why a mortgage lender would want to keep such an account for you: If they are loaning you tens of thousands of dollars, they surely don't want to take the chance that you might not pay your property taxes or insurance. They cover that risk by insisting that you give them a portion of those fees each month as part of your monthly payment.

When you buy a property any time other than at the beginning of the year, there should already be some money saved in the escrow account. If there is a positive balance in that account, you can have the seller assign it to you; if the balance is negative, you can insist that the seller bring the account current with his own funds. To do so, include this clause in your purchase offer:

> *Impounded or escrow funds, if any, for future payment of taxes, fire, casualty, flood and mortgage insurance, etc., as shown on mortgagee's statement(s) as approved by Buyer, are to be adjusted as a credit to the Seller and a debit to the Buyer. If there is a negative balance in the impound/escrow account, Seller shall bring the account current.*

Final Inspection

Your last inspection of the property should be just before closing. If the property hasn't been taken care of, or if agreed-upon repairs haven't been effected by the seller, it may be your last chance to take care of the problem.

The difficulty is usually invited by the buyer who allows the seller to make verbal promises without getting them in writing. A contract for the sale of real property must be *in writing*, and you are only asking for trouble when you take the seller's word that he will replace the broken windows in the basement.

Any repairs that the seller has agreed to effect before the closing should be specified in the contract, but you still can't be sure things will be taken care of. To ensure the needed repairs, include in the contract a clause that will keep a portion of the proceeds in an escrow account until the repairs are completed. If the seller has lived up to his side of the deal by the closing date, there won't be a problem. If he hasn't, there won't be a problem then either, because he cannot touch his money until he has taken care of the repairs.

You should *always* walk through the property on the day of the closing. Too many buyers have been very unpleasantly surprised *after* the closing—and then their only remedy is a lengthy and costly court case.

The Closing

At the end of the escrow period is the *closing*. It takes place when and where the buyer and seller agree. Traditionally, it is the seller who decides the place of the closing; however, you, as the buyer, can include in your offer a clause that will specify where and when the closing is to take place.

> *Closing shall take place on* _____
> *and shall occur at a location designated by the*
> *Purchaser.*

More than once I have been in a situation where my client and the seller and I all live in the same city, but the seller's attorney lives twenty miles away. If the purchaser failed to specify that the closing was to take place at my office, we all find ourselves on the road.

A closing does not have to take place at an attorney's office. It can be at a Realtor's office, or a title company's office, or in the broom closet at the local YMCA. (I wouldn't recommend the latter.) But if you know where you want it to take place, specify it in your offer.

To understand the closing better, you should realize that its primary function is to transfer title and (in most cases) possession to the buyer. The reason for all the formality and paperwork at closing becomes more apparent when you consider the importance of title.

Title, Title Search, and Title Insurance

Title is the formal right of ownership of property. We could not function as a society if we didn't have a method for recognizing each other's rights of ownership. If Fred and Bill both claim ownership of the same bottle of 7-Up, who gets to drink it? Well, if the case ever gets to court, one of them will have to prove that he has title to the soda. A sales receipt will probably work well enough. But when Fred and Bill both claim that they own the same three-bedroom house in Hometown, USA, we may have a serious problem.

To prevent such disputes—and to give property owners the peace of mind that comes from knowing that they legally and lawfully possess their property—we the people have come up with laws that govern ownership and title.

Possession of and title to a particular piece of property can be traced back to an original grant of that property to an individual by the federal or state government. From that time to the present, ownership has been conveyed through a legal instrument called a deed. For a deed to be valid, it must meet the following criteria:

1. It must include the names of the buyer (called the grantee) and the seller (the grantor).
2. A statement that shows the seller's intent to convey the title, such as "I convey, bargain, sell, or grant."
3. A description of the property.
4. The signatures of all grantors.
5. Delivery of the deed.

Different types of deeds carry with them different warranties. A General Warranty Deed includes covenants that guarantee that the seller has title and power to convey the property; that there are no liens or encumbrances other than those stated in the contract; and that the buyer will not be disturbed in his or her possession of the property by the seller or any third party. Of all deeds, a Quit Claim Deed warrants the least. It merely conveys to the buyer whatever interest the seller had in the property; if a problem comes up later, the buyer will have no recourse from the seller.

A deed should be recorded with the county government, giving public notice that the property has been conveyed. Without this recording, an unscrupulous seller could sell a piece of property to several buyers. If a deed is not recorded and the seller does attempt to convey the property to another buyer, that second buyer may very well prevail over the first buyer simply because the original deed was never recorded. By recording the deed, any subsequent buyers are put on notice that the title has been transferred and they cannot claim that they were unaware of the sale, since it was a matter of public notice.

It is through this one document that we are able to say with surety who the owner of a property is, and with the recording of deeds we can trace the history—the chain of title—of any property in the United States.

The title search (or title examination) will be performed during the escrow period for the buyer by his or her attorney, or by an escrow agent, the broker, or a title insurance company. The person searching the title will examine every record that has been filed with the county pertaining to the piece of property being sold. Records have been kept for many years—even centuries—and searching the chain of title allows the buyer to determine whether the seller has the right to convey that title.

Since any liens or encumbrances must be recorded, the examiner can find any defects in the title and report them to the buyer. The examiner, after searching the title thoroughly, will prepare an abstract of title, a list of all the records having to do with the property. The examiner will then give an opinion about the condition of the title.

A title company will, for an extra fee, insure the title searched by their employee against any hidden defects. The cost may seem like an unnecessary expense, especially at a time when the buyer is trying to save as much money as possible, but that policy protects the buyer in case someone suddenly appears with better title.

You should know exactly how much a title search and title insurance will cost before you incur these fees. Title companies charge different rates for their services, so shop around.

Closing Costs

Closing costs are fees paid at closing by the buyer and seller. I can't give you a specific breakdown of those costs and who will pay them because settlement costs can vary widely. Let me offer two bits of advice about closing costs, and then I'll give you a general list of common costs that you can find out about.

First, almost all closing costs can be paid by the buyer, or the seller, or split in any way they choose. While there are costs traditionally borne by either the buyer or seller, it is up to the parties to agree. Therefore, if you are negotiating with the seller and find that you reach a stalemate, offer to cover more (or less) of the closing costs in exchange for a lower (or higher) price.

Second, you can find out within a few dollars exactly what your closing costs will be just by asking your attorney (or title officer, banker, broker) in advance. They have had experience with closings and can give you a definite answer. Also, in case you are getting a new loan, the lender is required by law to give you an estimate of closing costs within three days of receiving your application.

Here are some of the closing costs that you may be responsible for:

Assumption fees are charged by the lender when you assume the seller's loan.

Appraisal fees pay for the appraisal that the lender will insist on before making the loan to you.

Points, as discussed before, are percentage points charged by the lender to make up for a low interest rate on the loan itself. For example, if the lender charged two points on a $60,000 loan, you would have to pay $1,200—in cash—at the closing.

Attorney's fees for handling the legalities of the transaction.

Recording fees are charged by the local government for recording the transfer of title and filing all the proper paper work.

Title insurance, which the lender usually insists on and I always recommend, is usually paid for by the buyer at closing. I also recommend that you obtain your own owner's title insurance policy.

Title search is generally paid by the seller, but. like any closing cost, is negotiable.

There will be other fees, such as notary fees and other miscellaneous expenses, which will be charged to the buyer and seller at the closing. The most important thing to remember is that you will have to come up with the correct amount—usually in cash or a cashier's check—on the day of the closing, so you should find out before then how much you will need to have. And *do* negotiate with the seller who will pay the assorted fees before you sign the contract. You can save yourself hundreds of dollars—in cash—by doing so.

Taking Possession

As a rule, possession will occur at the time of closing. However, there have been many cases where surprised and disgruntled sellers and buyers have not prepared in advance and possession has been delayed.

The problem usually comes up after a picture-perfect closing. The buyer has brought the money and signed every document in triplicate. The seller has signed his Warranty of Deed and Bill of Sale and every other shred of legal-looking paper pushed at him. The buyer has qualified for the new loan and has been approved, but suddenly, at closing, the lender is unwilling to disburse the funds to the seller. The bank officer smugly informs the parties that the bank must first check for impending liens and intervening liens, but that the funds will be disbursed within five working days.

That might not be a cataclysmic problem in all cases, but in many cases the seller was ready to take his money and move out, and the buyer was waiting to move in on the day of closing. Now the buyer is stuck with a moving van full of furniture and nowhere to move because the seller isn't ready to relinquish possession.

The solution is to find out in advance when the funding will take place. Every lender will have a different set of rules, and it won't be a problem if you will just ask in advance. The clause that you should include in your offer is: Possession shall occur at (closing/funding).

After the flurry of document signing and fee paying, the closing will be magically over. And in that magical moment you will joint the ranks of real estate investors, on your way to the fulfillment of your dreams. It will be nerve-wracking the first time, perhaps, but oh so worth it when you enter your first investment property.

Chapter Nine Summary

  I. The escrow period is the time between acceptance of the offer and the closing. It is a period for title searches, final inspections, obtaining the loan, and checking every detail twice. It can be as long or as short as the buyer and seller agree.

 II. You should inspect the property prior to closing. If any problems emerge during this inspection, take care of them immediately.

III. The closing is when all of the documentation is prepared and signed, all fees are paid, and title is transferred to the buyer. The closing can take place anywhere the buyer and seller agree.

IV. The owner of real property has title that can be transferred to another person by sale, exchange, or gift. Because of the importance of title, title companies were created to search the chain of title and insure that title against hidden liens or claims against it. The cost of owner's title insurance is money well spent.

 V. Closing costs are fees for processing the closing. These costs are paid for by the buyer and seller as per their agreement. Some closing costs may be:
   a. assumption fee
   b. appraisal fee
   c. points
   d. attorney's fees
   e. recording fees
   f. title search
   g. title insurance

There will be other costs as well; ask for a written estimate of closing costs prior to the day of closing.

VI. Traditionally, the buyer will take possession of the property at the time of closing; however, you can specify the transfer of possession in your purchase offer to be sure.

Chapter Nine Homework

1. There's only one homework assignment I could possibly give you at the end of the book: Get out there and buy at least one piece of investment property. I've given you what you need to get started, and I've shown you several experts who can help you with the details. Do the following at least once for a grade in this class:

   a. Get to know property values in at least one good investing area.

   b. Using one of the methods described in the book, find at least one house that appears to be a good deal.

   c. Prepare a tentative long-range plan for the proposed investment, and evaluate its possible profitability.

   d. Inspect the property carefully, looking for any defects. Cosmetic fix-ups are OK, but watch out for major repairs.

   e. Negotiate with the sellers, watching for needs not wants. Find out how strongly they are motivated to sell. How much downpayment do they really need? Can they lend you part of their equity? Do they have a low-interest assumable loan?

   f. If it still looks like a good deal, have it professionally appraised.

g. Make your final long-range plans. If it still looks profitable, present a written offer (don't forget the escape clauses).

h. Tentatively arrange for financing. You won't want to pay for loan application fees until after your loan is accepted, but you should definitely have financing lined up.

i. Upon acceptance of the offer, have the property professionally inspected. Have the title searched (you'll be required to do this) and purchase owner's title insurance. Apply for financing.

j. Get a written estimate of closing costs and have a cashier's check ready for the big day. What more do you need to do?

And it all makes perfect sense, doesn't it?

Conclusion

You Can Do It: The Financial Freedom Plan

"When you wish upon a star, makes no difference
who you are. . . ."

I have several wishes, and I hope they all come
true:

> I wish you health, happiness, and
> prosperity.
> I wish you to remember that the
> wealthy have the same problems
> you and I have, so prepare now.
> I wish for peace on earth.
> I wish you success and the fulfill-
> ment of your dreams.
> I wish that you will keep in mind
> the golden rule and let it guide your
> actions as you invest.
> I wish for you to **buy right.**

More than wish for you, I'm going to give you
a step-by-step plan that will assure your financial
freedom. I call it the Financial Freedom Plan. If

you will follow it for ten years (about one-fifth an average person's working life) it will give you:

Financial Independence

Tax-Free Income

A Hedge Against Inflation

Growth of Capital

Retirement Income

Family Security

Estate Liquidity

How can one plan do all of that? Just watch this:

For the plan to work you will have to buy three houses per year, paying an average of $75,000 for each (not an especially hard task, once you've begun to apply the techniques I've given you for finding and financing property). Second, there must be an average of 7.5 percent inflation for the next ten years. I think the average will be higher—much higher—but I can't believe it will be any lower, despite currently falling oil prices. Housing will continue to appreciate, the price of oil notwithstanding. Also, you must put only 5 percent down on each house purchased.

Here are the figures (approximate, depending on the factors mentioned above):

Year	Value of Houses Purchased	
1	$ 475,213	
2	440,980	
3	409,212	
4	379,732	
5	352,376	
6	326,991	
7	303,435	
8	281,575	
9	261,291	
10	242,467	
Total:	$3,473,272	(value of all thirty houses purchased in ten years)

How much will you still owe at the end of ten years?

$225,000 (3 @ 75,000) × 10 years
=

$2,250,000 original purchase price.
− 112,500 5% down payments

2,137,500
− 106,875 5% paydown on loans

$2,030,625 still owing

How much equity will you have in the thirty properties?

$3,473,272 value of real estate
−2,030,625 still owing

$1,442,647 equity

What is the average value per house?

$3,473,272 / 30 houses = $115,776

THE FREEDOM PLAN:

Sell eighteen homes and keep the other twelve (sell 60 percent of all the homes bought over the ten-year period and keep the other 40 percent).

18 homes sold × $115,776 (average value) = $2,083,968
Pay off all underlying loans currently owed: −2,030,625

Overage (to cover all selling costs):   53,343

What will you have left?

VALUE: 12 homes owned free and clear

($115,776 × 12) = $1,389,312

You can either keep and manage the dozen houses yourself, collecting the rental income and banking it, or you can sell all twelve at market value ($1,389,312) and reinvest the money in an instrument such as a C.D. Even if you only earn 10 percent on your money, you'll enjoy a healthy retirement income of $138,931 per year—without touching your capital.

And that's financial freedom!

Getting Started—
Taking the Initiative

J. P. Morgan once said, "Nobody ever became a millionaire without taking a chance." I've found that to be true. You won't *ever* buy real estate unless you make a written offer; you won't *ever* make a written offer unless you find a good deal; and you won't *ever* find a good deal unless you get out there and *look*. Take the chance; what have you got to lose?

As I travel around the country teaching people how to invest in real estate, I'm amazed at how many of them go to seminar after seminar, learning and learning but never investing. I always wonder, "What are they waiting for?"

I read in a periodical about a gentleman who lived in Colorado. A flood had hit the town, and as he stood on his front porch watching the swirling water, it began to creep up around his ankles, then his knees. A young man in a row boat paddled by and called out, "Climb in. I'll take you to higher ground."

"No thanks," the home owner yelled back. "I have faith in the Lord and He will save me."

About a half hour later he was still standing on the porch, clinging to the post as the water swirled around his chest. Another man came by in a motor boat and tossed him a rope. "Hang on, I'll pull you in to safety!"

"No thanks. I have faith in the Lord, and He will save me!"

An hour later he was on the roof, desperately hanging onto the chimney as the water threatened to cover him completely. A helicopter came by and hovered overhead. A rope ladder was tossed out and a voice boomed, "Climb up and we'll save you!"

"No thanks," once again. "The Lord will save me!"

Well, the waters closed over his head, and he found himself face-to-face with the Lord. "Lord," he cried, "why didn't You save me? I had such great faith in You!"

"What did you want from me?" the Lord replied. "I sent you two boats and a helicopter!"

In this book I've given you at least a half dozen boats and maybe one or two helicopters. If you don't make it as an investor, look at yourself. Your teachers can only do so much, and then it's up to you. Don't be like the seminar junkies I meet every day, who have certainly learned enough about real estate to get started, but who are still waiting for someone to take them by the hand and save them. It just doesn't work that way.

Remember the little train, and turn your "I think I can" into "I did it!"

Continue your education *while* you put what you've learned to use in the real world. Use the information you've picked up between the covers of this book. Get out there and BUY RIGHT.

And let me hear from you. I want to know about any success you've enjoyed and about any problems you've faced. When you are financially independent, I'll expect you to invite me out to dinner to thank me.

Index